T0065745

HOME WATERS

WATERS

FISHING WITH AN OLD FRIEND

JOSEPH MONNINGER

Broadway Books
New York

BROADWAY

A hardcover edition of this book was originally published in 1999 by Chronicle Books. It is here reprinted by arrangement with Chronicle Books.

HOME WATERS. Copyright © 1999 by Joseph Monninger. All rights reserved. No part of this book may be reproduced or transmitted in any form or by any means, electronic or mechanical, including photocopying, recording, or by any information storage and retrieval system, without written permission from the publisher. For information, address: Chronicle Books, 85 Second Street, San Francisco, CA 94105.

Broadway Books titles may be purchased for business or promotional use or for special sales. For information, please write to: Special Markets Department, Random House, Inc., 1540 Broadway, New York, NY 10036.

BROADWAY BOOKS and its logo, a letter B bisected on the diagonal, are trademarks of Broadway Books, a division of Random House, Inc.

Visit our website at www.broadwaybooks.com

First Broadway Books trade paperback edition published 2000.

Designed by Julia Flagg

Library of Congress Cataloging-in-Publication Data
Monninger, Joseph.
Home waters: fishing with an old friend / Joseph Monninger.
p. cm.
Originally published: San Francisco, CA : Chronicle Books, 1999.
1. Fly fishing—West (U.S.)—Anecdotes. 2. Dogs—Anecdotes.
3. Monninger, Joseph. I.
Title.
SH464.W4 M57 2000
636.752'7—dc21
00-024600

ISBN 978-0-767-90515-2

for **WENDY**

TABLE OF CONTENTS

1	Nellie	13
2	Where Dogs Come From	23
3	The Winds	43
4	Warm Springs	61
5	Yellowstone	83
6	Idaho	99
7	The Sun River	125
8	The Bighorn River	143
9	Tongue River	159
10	The North Platte	171
11	New Hampshire	181

To be successful, fly fishers must live in a floating world away from the routine duties and schedules of life. They adjust to the flow of the water, the way of the trout. They are wholly preoccupied with finding a fish that will, for a few minutes, join them in the dance. It is a ballet between partners — angler and fish — and set to the pace of the fly above and the trout below. The water moves, but the world stops.

M.R. MONTGOMERY, *THE WAY OF THE TROUT*

Any of us who has owned a dog that has taken a particular hold on our heart has dwelt on the unfairness of allocated time. It seems but an instant—or at best a couple of good gunning seasons—and the puppy we so carefully carried home and placed on the rug by our bed has suddenly become a little dim of eye, a touch slow to get up in the morning, and more and more content to lay in some sunny spot and salute our passings-by with a turning of the head and a wagging of the tail. Somehow even through the dozen dogs I've owned I've never ceased to be surprised and a little hurt to discover that today Tippy or Ben or Judy doesn't race me to the door to go out but stands in the warmth of the kitchen and merely follows me with eyes and heart.

GENE HILL, *FRED*

NELLIE

1:

IN THE SPRING OF 1997 I took my eleven-year-old Golden Retriever, Nellie, to see the vet. I had noticed a series of lumps under her skin, the lumps particularly dense along her spine. Goldens are notorious for troublesome skin, but Nellie has always been a beautiful dog with a gorgeous coat and clear eyes. In the decade I had lived with her, she had been sprayed by skunks, quilled by porcupines, even attacked by a pit bull, but she had never been ill. I didn't like the feel of the lumps. One particularly large lump rested beneath her right front leg, up where a human's lymph node might be located. Cancer, I thought, then tried to push the thought away. The next day I watched her when she ran or walked and I checked to make sure she ate her food. She seemed healthy enough, although somewhat sluggish. When I took her on our daily walk she did not dart off through the ferns and pucker brush that border my New Hampshire house. She stayed beside me, seemingly content to take a short walk and return home. She made it back before I did and remained stationary at the door, waiting to be let inside.

The night before the appointment, I called Nellie into bed and pulled her up close to me. It was April, still plenty cold at night, but I had the window cracked near the head of the bed. Wind skittered beneath the sash, carrying the raw, syrup smell of approaching spring in New England. It was a good smell. I kept the bedside lamp on for a while, then I turned it off and pulled Nellie closer, her large back spooned against me. I rubbed her chest. I tickled the top of her snout, an old thing between us, then pet her soft head. She didn't fall asleep at once. She grunted and made low, murmuring sounds. Burrs stuck to her belly, small sticks, too, and I pulled them away and kept brushing her until her breathing matched mine.

Before that moment, before having Nellie in bed beside me, I admit I had taken her, if not for granted, at least as an immutable part of my life. She was a fact in my daily activities. Wake up, feed her, walk her, check her water. Noon, when possible, sneak home from my teaching job and give her a walk. Saturday mornings we loaded my Dodge Dakota pickup with our week's garbage, then headed to the Bridgewater Town dump. Nellie rode beside me, and where a pasture stretched to a string of peaks bordering Newfound Lake, I let her out and threw a Nylabone Frisbee a thousand, maybe ten thousand, times to her. And because the pasture sloped gently downward, I could throw the Frisbee for fifty yards or more and watch her streak through the timothy grass and beard's tongue, her fur dazzling in the bright Saturday light.

Eleven years. That's what I thought about as I pet her in the darkness. She had come to live with me in 1986, when I was married, and she had seen me through a divorce, through the beginning of a new start at teaching, through the sale of one home and the purchase of a new one, through days of wood cutting, through a summer on the Crow Reservation in Montana, through hundreds of hikes through the White Mountains, through swims in the ocean and lakes of New England and Canada, and through nights when sadness or depression closed in and I could wait and count on the quiet dip of the bed, the soft, comforting curl of her coming to rest beside me. She was so much a part of my life that at my office, without Nellie around, I often spoke to air, inadvertently mistaking the sound of a furnace coming on or a student's key chain for the rattle of her collar as she made her way to me. Nell, I'd say, and only realize after the word was formed that she wasn't nearby.

Suddenly that presence was in jeopardy. I knew, lying next to her, that I was frightened for myself at least as much as for Nellie. I needed the steadiness of her demands, the consistency she brought to my life. I couldn't imagine days without her. So that night in bed I stayed close to her and whispered in her ear that she was a good girl, a Frisbee catcher, a lake swimmer. I told her she had to get well, that she couldn't let cancer take hold of her. She snored in response and I fell asleep some time later, a rain waking us in the morning.

At first light we walked down to a creek behind the house. She wandered through the woods, the green leaves pushing from the birches almost translucent. She liked to be out in the morning, I knew. We stopped at Clay Brook and she had a long drink. Front legs flexed, her steady pink tongue lapping at water, she kept an eye ready for any movement in the woods. I picked up scraps of pine kindling and bundled them against my chest.

When I had a full load, I whistled her up to head back. She kept drinking for a little longer, then pushed away from the stream and trotted through the woods. I saw her intermittently as the trees obscured her passage, her gold fur visible one moment, then blending with the early sun the next. When I reached my yard, she came up behind me with a stick. It was an established game between us: she snuck up and let the stick touch my hand and I grabbed it quickly. Then she could lunge back, growling, pretending we were in the fight of a lifetime. She shook her head back and forth, the stick whacking against my thighs. Then it was my job to say okay, it's yours, and pretend disinterest. She trotted back and stuck the stick in my hand and the game continued until I told her it was enough for one day.

I stacked the kindling on the porch and told her it was time to get going. She dropped the stick and came inside. I gave her a biscuit at the kitchen sink and she gave me her paw. For some reason she had always given me her paw after the biscuit, not before as most dogs do. I found it a more honest exchange and told her so. She went to lie on her dog bed while I got ready for the day. Her eyebrows flexed up and down as she watched me move around the house. When at last I asked if she wanted to go for a ride, she beat me to the door. She hopped into my pickup, glad to be going for a ride on a spring day.

Dr. Sweet is a large, comfortable man who holds a veterinarian's degree from Kansas State. His office is located in a converted New England Cape in Rumney, New Hampshire. Standing beside him as he examined Nellie, I tried to read his face. I couldn't say for certain what he was thinking, though he seemed intent, focused in a way he might not be for an ordinary visit. He took her temperature and said it was normal. He checked her ears, her teeth, then ran his hands back and forth over the lumps. He asked me about their derivation, when I had first noticed them, how fast they had grown. I told him I had felt them now and then, but they had never pushed as hard against her skin, I said, as they seemed to now. He spent two or three minutes lifting Nellie's leg to examine the lump beneath her armpit. He explained that Goldens often get fatty cysts, that lumps didn't mean that she had cancer, but that he thought they should probably come out anyway. He said he worried about putting older dogs under sedation, but that because she seemed healthy, it might be worth it to get the lumps out and take a look. He said if the lumps came back, then we would have to start worrying.

"In fact, we could do it now," he said. "I've got a free surgery block today."

It happened that fast. A few minutes later, I handed Nellie's lead over to Dr. Sweet's assistant, a young woman who had worked several years for him. She explained that they would keep Nellie overnight, that I could call at four to get an update on her condition, that someone would check on her during the night, and that I could pick her up first thing the following morning if everything went well. She also warned me that they would probably have to shave a good deal of Nellie's fur, that I should be prepared to see her looking a little grim the next day. Then she held the leash while I squatted and gave Nellie a quick pet. When I stood, Nellie scrambled on the linoleum to come with me. The assistant checked her with a tug, then took her back to cage her. True to her nature, once she understood what was expected of her, Nellie didn't resist.

Back in my truck, I found my hands were shaking. I tried to dismiss the sadness, tried to think about other things. Just a dog, I reminded myself. Then, for the first time since I was a small boy, I started to sob. The cries came so quickly, and with such force, that I couldn't hold them back. I sobbed as I had not sobbed over the death of my father or mother, or over my divorce, though I would be quick to assure anyone that those human lives, that marriage, counted more on some humanistic scale than a Golden Retriever who stole dinner scraps from the counter or rolled in dead creatures to rob their scent. Still, I cried. Perhaps it was the notion that she was innocent. Perhaps it was the knowledge that she had never been false to me, that she depended and trusted me wholly and without doubt. It did no good, in the warmth of the pickup truck, to tell myself that it was foolish to feel so strongly about a dog. I loved her as truly, and as unselfishly, as I had loved anything in my life.

I had classes the rest of the day and student conferences, but at four I closed the door to my office and called Dr. Sweet. He wasn't able to come to the phone, but his assistant told me they had removed seventeen lumps, some quite large, from various spots around her body. Nellie was resting. She seemed fine and had taken the sedation well. She had been awake for an hour or two, had sipped from her water bowl, and had not worried the stitches at all. They were pleased with her condition so far. The assistant asked me if I wanted to send the tumors out for biopsy. She said they couldn't determine if the tumors were malignant or not without a biopsy. I told her no, I didn't think it mattered, that I wasn't going to authorize extensive surgery if she did have cancer and that it would probably be better not to know in any case. The assistant didn't seemed convinced, but I told her I was certain. She said I could think about it overnight. I promised I would.

The next morning I was at Dr. Sweet's office when it opened at eight o'clock. As soon as Nellie heard my voice, she started to whine from her crate. I settled the bill with the receptionist, then waited while she explained the dosage for the antibiotics they prescribed to fight infection. The assistant passed by the desk to get Nellie and she warned me again that they had shaved a good deal of her hair. I said I understood.

The front door of the office opened and a woman with a Pomeranian came in, the dog panting heavily for such a tiny creature. Then I heard Nellie's claws raking the linoleum as she pulled to escape from the back quarters of the office. The assistant said, "Whoa, Nellie," which is a common joke when anyone handles my dog. Nellie yanked around the corner and exploded into my hands. The assistant, I could tell, watched my reaction. The cuts and shaved parts were horrible. What before had been a magnificent coat was now pocked and degraded. The stitches stood out in black rows, thick as football laces, and it was difficult to lay your hands on her without touching an incision. I could tell immediately that she needed to walk because she refuses to go to the bathroom in cages or pens. As quickly as I could, I thanked everyone and hustled out the door, Nellie pulling as she does not usually pull. I took her across the driveway and let her do her business on a wide grassy field. When she started to roll, doubtless trying to rid herself of the stitches, I gathered her up and got her in my truck.

I took her to McDonald's. She loves cheeseburgers. Sitting on the tailgate of my pickup, Nellie beside me, I fed her the cheeseburger and tried to see the damage to her skin and body. It was extensive, more extensive than I had dreamed possible. Although she ate with good appetite, snapping the cheeseburger from my fingers with loud, lippy chomps, something had changed. Whether the lumps were malignant or not—and I had confirmed my decision not to have them biopsied—Nellie was no longer a pup. I knew that, of course, and had understood it

19

intellectually for some time, but sitting on the tailgate, looking out at the scrubby field of brush and sumac behind the McDonald's, my dog was suddenly old. This dog, who had been dear to me for so long, whose only want in life was to be with me, was facing the first winds of her own death.

Overly dramatic, certainly. I knew that. But I realized — for whatever psychological reasons others cared to apply — that I was one of those people who feel a connection with an animal beyond what others might consider normal. Sitting on the tailgate of the truck, the cheeseburger gone and my arm up to hold her head on my shoulder, I decided that I wanted to take a last trip with Nellie. I wanted to go out West, to Wyoming and Montana, to fly fish the streams I loved and to have Nellie with me. I wanted her to see bison and elk again, to wade in cold Western streams, to run across open mountain passes. I knew that it was probably foolish, that to think of a dog in such terms meant that I was guilty of the worst kind of anthropomorphic attribution. At the same time, though, I knew Nellie, knew what made her happy, knew what made her bright and interested. And more than that, I knew I owed her something, that the fidelity and love she had shown me throughout her life deserved acknowledgment. If she was going to die from a cancer that might take her body, I wanted to know that I did what I could do to make her remaining time joyous. That was the bargain we struck on the tailgate behind McDonald's. It was the reason we headed west for a month of fly-fishing.

We could not leave right away, however. Nellie needed to mend, for one thing, and I had commitments throughout the spring and summer. We aimed to leave in September, immediately after Labor Day, hoping to miss the crowds by doing so. I spent a happy summer collecting travel maps, outlining the fishing trip, and getting my tackle in order. I tried to keep my equipment to a minimum, but, as always happens, my inventory list soon filled with a float tube, waders, two fly rods—a five-weight and a nine-weight—a cook stove, pots and pans, heavy clothes for the chilly nights I would encounter, and a bathing suit in case it became warm. I brought along my flytying kit. I brought three flashlights, a tent, a sleeping cot, matches of all kinds, bug spray, a baseball hat, flannel shirts, boots, Tevas, and water jugs. I filled a plastic chest with peanut butter and jelly, tomato soup, beans and rice, and cold cereal. I loaded a purple plastic vat with Nellie's food, a Frisbee, a brush, and three leashes. I arranged everything in my living room, circling the couch little by little, until eventually I knew I could take no more without risk to my truck.

As soon as word leaked out that I was leaving, and that I was going on a prolonged fishing trip, fisher-friends began calling and giving recommendations. One knew of a place in Wyoming. Another had a secret lake in Montana. I took down every suggestion and, gradually, began to see that it was possible to make a lazy U that would bring me along Route 80 from the south, bend up 287 through Wyoming, follow the Wind River Range in a kind of hypotenuse, hit Yellowstone, fish a place I knew in Idaho, then travel up to the Sun River in Montana, bend down on Route 90, hit the Tongue River, a few streams in middle Montana, then finish in what is arguably the best fishing in the West—the Big Horn River. I immediately liked the symmetry of the trip. I knew that by mid-October it would be too cold to camp comfortably night after night and I preferred, if possible, to be heading east by then. It may have made more sense to start on the northern leg first, but a dear friend of thirty years, Bob Harvey, caught the traveling bug when he heard about the trip and agreed to meet me in the Wind Rivers to hike in to some of the alpine lakes where the fishing, we knew from experience, is incomparable. We agreed to rendezvous in Lander, Wyoming, to hike a trail called Bears Ear, and to fish what we could fish. Bob added that his brother-in-law, Tom, might be persuaded to join us.

I spent the night before our departure making calls and arranging last minute details. I checked my fishing tackle again. Then I made sure I had the maps, the flashlights, the sleeping bag. Check and double check. Finally I sat at my dining room table and did little more than look out the window where my backyard lay illuminated under a floodlight. As always happens before I leave on a journey, my home seemed especially dear: the sound of the refrigerator coming on and off, the click of the furnace, the clink of heat ticking through the registers.

I checked Nellie before going to bed. Her lumps had not returned. Her fur had grown back, covering the stitches and making her coat wonderful again. I put her through her tricks. I made her give me her paw, sit, down-stay, then heel. She did everything I asked. I gave her a couple of biscuits from the kitchen, and then told her it was time to go to sleep. She jumped into bed with me, and huffed a little as she curled up for the night. We lay quiet for a while and listened to the house close down for sleep. I felt nervous and excited, ready to go. The acorns kept twanging off the roof, autumn already here.

WHERE DOGS COME FROM

2:

DOGS ARE A STANDING INTRODUCTION. I knew that once, but had forgotten it somewhere along the line. A man traveling alone in a pickup truck wearing khaki shorts and a baseball cap is often the object of suspicion. But a man traveling with an attractive dog, and a clear intent to fish, is another matter altogether. The first night out, at Lake Erie State Park in western New York, I tied Nellie to a long lead attached to the picnic table in our small camping spot. I fed her, gave her water, then busied myself setting up sleeping arrangements. It's a distinct pleasure, and a bit disorienting, to find yourself putting into practice what you had planned for months beforehand. Although I had brought a tent along, my design was to sleep in my truck on an old cot that I had packed for that purpose. To make room, however, I had to unload nearly everything and pile it on top of the fiberglass truck cap or squeeze it into the front cab. Before five minutes had passed, I realized I had turned my truck into what used to be known in California as a surfing safari wagon. With an inflated float tube on top, plastic vats of dog food and cereal, waders, flippers, a box containing my flytying gear, I was clearly designated as a man going fishing. Even the campground host, who had taken my ten dollars and pointed me to the appropriate tent slot, swung by again on his golf cart and asked where I was going fishing, how long I would be out. When I told him my idea for the trip, he related some of his own fish stories, again providing me with a place that couldn't miss, a place where the trout did the back stroke and waited to oblige fishermen.

But it was Nellie who made the most friends. At the end of her lead, she stretched to sniff the hands of a pack of children who came by, their fingers coated with marshmallow goo. In the campfire dimness, the children circled her and spoiled her, then ran off to wash for bed. Their place was taken by an older woman who passed with a towel around her neck and a flowered shower kit in her hand. She was at least sixty, apparently alone; I had seen her sitting at her own picnic table beside a minivan with Wisconsin plates. Switching her shower kit into her left hand, she bent to pet Nellie, who continued to strain at the end of her lead. When the woman stood, she said to me, "Nice dog." Then she shifted her towel around her neck again.

That was all it took. Nellie had served to introduce us, and for the next half hour the woman, whose name was Ronnette, kept one hand on my dog's back, the other on her towel. She told me she was on her way to visit her granddaughter, brand new, who had been born three weeks before. She said she was going to Massachusetts, heading the other way, east to my west, and she had considered flying but it had been years since she had taken a long drive and, besides, she actually liked to camp a little. She had camped often with her husband, Ben, who had died three years ago. They had owned a collie once, a black and white one, not a brown and white one like Lassie, and it had been a wonderful dog, but prone to chewing, especially when left alone.

Nellie gave her complete attention to Ronnette, except when the children passed by and again fussed over her. When the children departed, Ronnette said that her collie, KoKo, had died a long time ago, probably somewhere in the middle eighties. Then she thought about it for a second and tried to remember exactly, performing that curious exercise that dogs seem to draw out of people. Dogs, I knew, were about time. For most people a dog recalled a specific period, and I would find, throughout my trip, that people who encountered Nellie told me about their own dogs, then inevitably remembered the dog's death. And when the people spoke about their dog's ending, they almost always kept one hand on Nellie, their eyes looking off in the distance.

When Ronnette went back to her camp, I spent a little while tying flies. I am an atrocious flytier, but I like the idea of doing it even if I am ham-handed. Besides, I needed to replenish my fly box. I clamped my vise to the picnic table and began tying my specialty, a triple-hackled trico. It's my specialty because it is the simplest fly a person can tie. After wrapping glitter around the stem of the hook, I topped the shank with three hackles. The hackles go on in a straightforward manner — dark, white, dark. The triple hackle, in addition to being a simple fly to tie, represents nearly anything moving in the water. It is as close as one can come to a universal fly. I tied it in the darkness by the light of a headlamp. The poor lighting might have been an excuse for a better flytier, but my flies came out as poorly as they always did. Nellie wandered around at the end of her lead. The campground grew more quiet. I finished four

flies before calling it a night. By then the campfires had
begun to die and I smelled their sweet fragrance, the scent of
an encampment. Now and then I saw the silhouettes of
people standing in their tents, preparing for bed. The crickets
hardly spoke.

I took Nellie for a final walk. She is good about such things.
I can say "last walk" and she knows it is time to be serious. We
walked through the campground, then wandered over to a wide
patch of grass. The grass led to a meadow, which in turn led to
a group of power line stanchions. From there, I figured, you
could walk for miles.

At a safe distance from the campground, I let her off her
lead. She walked with the high-gaited step she sometimes uses
when the grass is wet. She inspected the hedgerow, the dense
dam of bushes that pushed out from the uncut patches of
growth. She has always liked, as most dogs do, the green tidal
zone where forest meets meadow. She spent a few minutes
sniffing and wading through the olive-colored grass. She looked
beautiful in the meadow, the moonlight picking her up enough
to reveal her fine coat, the white puff of a tail. She found a certain bush that held her interest, then she gave it up and circled
around until she concluded her nightly chores. We stood for a
while afterward and looked around. Someone once told me that
Charles Darwin speculated that eighty percent of the planet's
population does not lift its eyes above the horizon once a day.
Whether true or not, whether Darwin ever said it or not, the
quote has stuck in my brain and I have made it my routine to
look up at least once every twenty-four hours. More often than
not, I use my last walk with Nellie each night to survey the
stars. I have learned the stars' names, at least some of them, a
hundred different times, but invariably I forget them a month

later. I know the North Star. I know a few of the planets. But I have decided, in recent years, that it is okay to fail at the constellations, consoling myself that names don't change the nature of a thing. The stars don't alter no matter what we call them, so now, when people from the cities visit, I tell them all manner of nonsense, inventing names on the spot.

Nellie, I have noticed, rarely looks above the horizon. I am not sure she has ever done so in her life. I have tried, at various times, to get her interested in a stellar phenomenon—I wondered, for example, if she would have any reaction to Hale-Bopp—but she appears to be oblivious. Standing next to her in the field, I let my hand dangle on her head. I rubbed the space between her eyes, then tickled the top of her skull. She sat and let me keep going. I played the childhood game of blinking my left eye to make the stars jump one way, then my right eye to make them jump the other way. By doing it quickly, I could force one star to leap over the point of a pine.

We went back to the truck. Nellie walked easily on her leash. I hooked her to the towing ball while I cleaned the picnic table. I packed up everything, stowing it as carefully as I could, and realized, as I did so, that much of traveling is fussing. I put what I could on the roof of the truck, keeping things off the ground and away from raccoons. I figured we would have a frost. It was likely I would have frost every night from now on.

When I finished wrapping up camp, I put down the tailgate and let Nellie leap in first. I had set up an L.L. Bean cedar dog bed next to the cot, but naturally she preferred my bed. She curled into a ball on top of my sleeping bag and tried to ignore me. She went limp on purpose, hogging everything, which is a terrible trick she likes to play. I climbed in and shoveled her off, but not without an awkward struggle. Eventually I yanked the tailgate up and we were in, buttoned up for the night. A nice breeze lifted off Lake Erie. This cot was home for the next month, I told Nellie, but she didn't appear to pay attention. I turned this way and that, settling in, adjusting to the sensation—familiar but always surprisingly constricting—of sleeping in a mummy bag.

I flicked on my headlamp and read a bit from *So Little Time* by John Marquand. I nearly always bring Marquand on camping trips, not only because I admire him so, but because his books are about martinis and weekends in other people's houses. His books are like portable black-and-white movies, the best kind, and nearly as important, they take time to read. You don't want a short, snappy book on a camping trip.

After a while I turned off the headlamp and put Marquand aside. For a time I stayed awake, nervous and eager, happy to be started but also aware that no one in the world knew where I was at that moment. I reached down and put my hand on Nellie's rising ribs. She rolled over to have her belly rubbed, but I was too tired to oblige her. I fell asleep to her paw gently cuffing my wrist, trying to get my hand started.

I was living with my wife, Amy, at the St. Paul's School in Concord, New Hampshire, when we decided to get a dog. It was August. Earlier that summer we had been house-sitting in Putney, Vermont, and our daily walk had taken us past a beautiful antique Cape with the requisite Golden Retriever outside. The retriever was old, and somewhat unsteady on her feet, but she invariably barked twice when we arrived, rose to a standing position, her back hips obviously arthritic, then tottered toward us, her tail going. It was a highlight of our walk, if not of our entire day. We didn't know the dog's name, but because she was so reticent to come forward, and because she barked at us every single day, one of us named her Shy Girl. The name stuck. From that point on, whenever we talked about the possibility of getting a dog, we talked about Shy Girl.

If dogs are about time, they are also about the romance of steadiness. In American mythology, dogs come with screen doors that slam, swing sets, leaf raking parties, and jack-o-lanterns. For many of us, we want the idea of a dog long before we want the dog itself. Shy Girl, although she was a loving dog and entirely wonderful in her own right, was also a symbol for us. We had met approximately ten years earlier and since then we had lived in Africa, Vienna, and New York. Our travel had been exciting, but we had failed to set roots. In our summers as teachers, we had led student groups to Australia, New Zealand, Canada, Holland, England, and France. Suddenly, however, we were thirty-five years old with a limited bank account, no permanent home, and a growing suspicion that we needed to settle into something lasting.

St. Paul's seemed to answer that need. Amy took a position as an English teacher, and as a dorm mom, while I taught as a visiting professor at the University of New Hampshire. We were given wonderful accommodations in Friendly House, the old converted servants' quarters, and were put in charge of forty or fifty girls. Amy was gifted as a student advisor. On dorm duty every second or third night, she made a fire in our living room, sat at an old oak table with her work spread in front of her, and counseled students, joked with them, talked about boys, took temperatures, and, in her quiet moments, wrote lavishly on their themes and papers.

I think, perhaps, we got a dog instead of having a child. I also think we knew, on some level, what we were doing, though neither one of us admitted it at the time. I'm certain the people around us, on hearing that we were getting a dog, probably rolled their eyes and said we should be having children instead. Looking back, I've often thought that we remained childless because we each silently suspected that we were not staying together. We told each other, surrounded by children, that we needed none of our own.

A dog was another matter. The arguments for a dog were compelling. St. Paul's has always been overrun with dogs. The school is set on an exquisite campus, approximately 118 acres of New Hampshire meadows, forests, and lakes. Faculty and staff tend to stay for years, giving the entire school a sense of continuity. When a groomer friend mentioned that a friend of a friend had just come into a first-rate litter of Golden Retrievers, we didn't hesitate. It was time for a dog.

On a bright September Saturday morning, the first chill of autumn making us sit outside and find the sun while we drank our coffee, we left St. Paul's to get Nellie. We had both had beagles as kids, Amy's dog named Cookie, mine named Porky, but that had been years ago. On the phone, the trainer had said we could have Brown Boy, a male, for $400. She said we could take a female for $200, but that the breeders required an agreement that the bitch not be neutered, and that the breeder got to pick the first and third pup from a litter. The trainer also said the breeders had a specialist supervising the dogs' breed characteristics, and that they would find a suitable mate after the female passed through two estrous cycles. We listened to all this information about reproduction half-heartedly. Against all advice to the contrary—new dogs owners generally do better with females because females tend to be less dominant—we wanted a male.

We drove along Route 7 to a beautiful farmhouse in southern New Hampshire and stepped out of the car to find a litter of Golden Retriever puppies wobbling around a spacious lawn. What had been a prospecting trip—maybe we'd get a dog, maybe we wouldn't—rapidly became a shopping trip. We were sunk. The puppies were ten weeks old and ridiculously cute. Brown Boy, when the trainer pointed him out, was a large, frumpy piece of fur. He was very sweet, but somehow, whenever we looked around, a small female seemed to be trailing us. She had a thinner face than Brown Boy, but she also seemed more alert. On our knees on either side of the pack, we asked the trainer to explain again the conditions for a female. She did. Then she left us alone to think about which dog we might like.

The dogs wandered between us, wrestling and sleeping almost at random, and we watched them closely. I wish that Amy and I had talked more about what was going on, what the dogs represented, but I suppose it is the nature of divorce that it has its beginnings in many things, not all of them knowable. Dogs are about time, as I've said, and at that time we wanted a dog. Neither of us was wise enough to look behind that desire.

Nellie was the one we wanted. Her official American Kennel Club name was Star Lake Nell. She came from a litter in Hanover, up near Dartmouth. We wrote a check, agreed to all the conditions concerning reproduction, then bundled her into the car. Amy drove and I kept Nellie entertained on my lap until she fell asleep. Her fur was soft and she smelled like doughnuts.

I read books on dog obedience and worked hard on making her sit, come, stay, heel. We crate-trained her. In the afternoons or the early evenings, we walked her all over the school grounds, going through the Pillsbury fields, the long trail along Turkey Pond, and even the trout stream in the center of campus. A young teaching intern named John had just acquired a black Lab puppy named Gusty, so we walked frequently with them, letting the dogs run and wrestle, their bodies nearly inexhaustible. If dogs did nothing else for us except force us to take to the fields and rivers in all kinds of weather, that would surely be enough.

It's likely I spent too much time with Nellie, that I relied too much on her companionship, because my wife and I had started to drift apart. In our continued effort to put down roots, an effort that would prove futile, we bought a century-old home on Port Hood Island, Nova Scotia. It had belonged to a lobster-man originally and had remained in his family for three genera-tions. Financially, it was a crazy move and caused incredible strain in our marriage. We lived fourteen hours of hard driving away from the house. We would have been far wiser to have purchased a house in northern New Hampshire where we might have had good weekends away from the confinement of prep school life, but our vision was that we would spend the summers at the island house, improving it gradually every year. Besides, the house overlooked the sea, with wide grass fields sloping down to an incredible blue. It was a place, we thought, to make a stand. We would teach in New Hampshire through the fall and spring, then spend glorious summers on an island of grass and ocean. The same house on the Maine coast, we liked to tell each other, would be worth several million dollars.

Nellie was part of that house. She came with us when we drove up that first summer. She was able to swim whenever she liked, dipping down to the ocean that ran up onto our land. During the hotter parts of the day, she sat in the shade, looking out at the birds and boats. I converted a fishing shed to a writing room, the old gray beams hung with lobster gear, and Nellie spent her mornings with me there, laying in the sunny doorway, tail ready to greet anyone who came by. In the evenings we played croquet with the kids on the island, Nellie constantly sneaking in to run off with one of the colorful balls. A picture of those evenings, with the island kids barefoot, the adults watching the game on Adirondack chairs, Nellie running freely, the sea everywhere, can still fill me with longing.

One morning in the middle of our first summer on the island, when Bert Smith, our local caretaker, and I were approximately a half mile out to sea checking his mackerel nets, I turned to look landward and saw a wake coming toward me. Occasionally we saw what the locals called "black fish," or harbor whales, and I told Bert we had one approaching. But when I looked again and squinted against the morning glare, I realized it was Nellie. She was nine months old. She had seen me go to sea, so she had gone to sea. She was swimming after me, her ears spread on the surface of the sea, her breathing a *chaaa chaaa chaaa,* her paws paddling endlessly through the swells. She had been swimming for the better part of an hour at least, her gaze fixed on me. We pulled her into the boat and I fussed over her while she shook off the water. Nellie, like most dogs, simply accepted that I had forgotten her, that she had rectified the situation, and now we could go on with the day. Watching her shake off in the sun, Bertie said he had seen deer sometimes swimming miles off shore, driven to the sea by insects, then swept out by currents. He said he had seen a deer go down that way, its antlers sinking below the surface until a last survival impulse pushed it up again, its antlers butting against heaven before it dropped finally into the sea water.

When I told Nellie's story later to a friend, she remarked that love, if it was anything, was the ability not to hesitate. She said Nellie had fetched her heart to me and that she would always find me wherever I went. She said the fact that Nellie did not think when she came to the water, did not weigh anything, but simply followed what she loved, was something, ultimately, to be envied.

We lost the island house in the divorce. On teachers' salaries, neither one of us was able to maintain a summer residence so far removed from our daily lives. We sold the house and divided our other property, including our pets. Amy took an old tomcat named Gray Man. I took Nellie. I had spent more time with her, had trained her, and, in some way, needed a dog in a way Amy did not. After thirteen years together, I moved out with the contents of one pickup truck, Nellie on the seat beside me.

Nellie and I arrived in Lander, Wyoming, at noon on our fourth day out. The entrance to Lander from the south is dramatic. The land turns red and begins to tuck closer to the road, forming a ruddy chute that drops from the plateau into a valley that contains the Wind River. At the brink of town, you begin to see fishing access signs. These signs are scattered all over the West. Brown and rectangular, with a white hook dangling in front of wide-eyed fish, they are somewhat torturous to pass, because each one seems promising. Fishermen use them to guide each other to good spots. Find the fishing access spot, then wade upstream, they will tell each other. I slowed as I passed each access point, not because I intended to fish them, but because I wanted to make mental notes. My short-term memory is abysmal and seems to get worse every year, but I have never had difficulties remembering fishing spots.

Nellie, when she felt the truck wind down at these signs, looked rapidly from me to the road. She had been a good sport about the traveling, taking our short breaks well and chasing the Frisbee if I threw it, but she was bored. Most mornings she slept with her chin on my knee, but in the afternoons she was restless. Now, with the truck slowing to examine the fishing signs, she stood, then sat, then stood again. Her nose rubbed the windshield from inside. It was already streaked with a thousand nose marks, but she found a few new spots to mark. It did no good, at this point, to tell her to relax. She wanted out and I didn't blame her. Suddenly, we had arrived. We had seen the sky opening for the last two days and now it was bright above us, wide in a way that it is never wide in the East.

I pulled over not next to the river, but on a small dirt road heading into what appeared to be a ranch pushed up against the Wind River Range. Side roads are always best for running a dog and this one promised to be excellent. A cattle grate covered the intersection of the dirt road and the interstate. On either side of the road, pale green sage spread for miles. As soon as I stopped the truck, I popped open the passenger door. Nellie flew off the seat, her body so eager to be moving she couldn't wait. By the time I climbed out, she was already down off the crest of the dirt road, her tail up, her nose skimming the ground. She galloped over the field, whisking through sage, her back legs impatient with her front legs, so desperate was she to run. Now and then she stopped and looked at me, apparently not trusting her luck that she was free to run as long as she liked. I told her to go. She didn't need to be told twice.

I opened the tailgate, pulled out sandwich fixings, and sat and watched. I had time to eat a peanut butter and jelly sandwich before she returned. She was winded. Her tongue lolled out of the right side of her mouth and her fur was dotted with burrs. I brushed her out, poured water for her, then gave her a couple of biscuits. She panted around, lapping the water and slopping things onto the dry ground before she finally found a spot in the shade under the tailgate. She flumped onto the dirt and reclined backward, happy to have a run, happy to be cool in the white soil. As always, it surprised me that she had no further expectation. If I had decided to stay the next two months in my truck, living on peanut butter and jelly and reading books on my tailgate, she would have remained gladly beside me. If I moved to Boston and decided to take a small apartment, she would have lived with me there.

We drove into town a little later. Lander, like many towns in the West, has undergone a conversion to the eco-trade, adventure travel business that sustains many western regions in a manner ranching would be hard pressed to match. The fleece economy, a friend of mine calls it, referring to the preferred clothing of the clients. NOLS, an organization for outdoor learning, is headquartered in Lander, and you can almost always spot the people who work there, most of them driving Jeeps and wearing expensive sunglasses. Lander's streets are wide and dotted with tourist shops selling postcards, disposable cameras, and Native American gear. There are also several taxidermy stores, some with signs saying they are willing to trade antlers. Signs throughout Wyoming tell you how far you are from Yellowstone, and Lander is no exception. Lander is not a destination anywhere near as popular as Yellowstone, but it is becoming more popular, which subjects it to the kind of Catch-

22 that threatens hot places for the fleece trade. Drawn to out-of-the-way places, the fleece trade invades an area until it becomes overrun by other fleece traders. Gradually, then, it becomes less interesting, less remote in the best sense, and becomes less appealing to a group of people who define themselves by the status gained by getting away from it all. The same principle, unfortunately, can often be applied to anglers.

Nellie and I had the afternoon to kill while we waited for my longtime friend and fishing buddy, Bob Harvey, and his brother-in-law, Tom, whom I had never met. I parked in the center of town and found a spot on a bench in the sun. The heat felt good. Nellie curled up in a shady spot nearly underneath the bench and pretended to sleep. I looked at my watch. Bob and Tom were arriving from Salt Lake City near five. I had at least three hours on my hands. After a while I walked over to The Good Place, an outdoor shop specializing in fishing and hunting. I tied Nellie to a pole outside and went in to browse the topo maps. I hate appearing like a sport, an easterner who has come out West on holiday, but it was unavoidable. Eventually one of the store clerks came over to help me. She said Bears Ear, the trail we intended to take the next day, was a great hike. She also said the Popo Agie River ran at the end of town and if I had an afternoon to kill, it wouldn't be a bad place to get out the kinks.

I paid for a license, which I needed anyway, then followed her directions out to the edge of town. Nellie guessed what was up and had the jitters at the thought of taking a swim. We found a brown sign that indicated fishing access and parked in a square dirt lot. The sun was still hot.

It took me a while to dig my fishing equipment out of the truck bed. Nellie, impatient for the water, kept running to the cattle fence that lined the bank, inspecting it, then running back to me. The water, when I looked in that direction, appeared a metal shelf, a glinting rigid blade stabbed through brown hills and brush.

It took ten minutes to get rigged up. I gave Nellie a biscuit that she hardly tasted. She wanted the water and that was all. When I slapped my thigh to tell her I was ready, she darted off and slipped under a strand of barbed wire, performing a GI crawl I didn't know she knew how to do. I carried a five-weight rod down to the river. As I approached, the water softened. It was no longer metal, but liquid instead, the melt of sun on rock and brown grasses. Crickets frittered up and into the light. Behind me black mountains stretched in a line toward the horizon. The land smelled of cattle and barns and corn.

Nellie waited for me chest deep in the river. She often ruins good fishing holes, but her company is worth it to me. I told her, though, that she would have to swim upstream or downstream but she didn't listen. She bent and lapped at the water, refreshed after our long days of driving.

The Popo Agie, the section on the outskirts of Lander, was small and beautiful. It rolled back and forth, twisting over farm country, bordered, in most places, by barbed wire fences. I walked downstream a bit until I found what appeared to be a particularly deep hole. I unhooked my fly, a black gnat, and cast. The water met the fly and carried it, as each river does, toward the sea.

I did not fish particularly well. I was too conscious of my surroundings, of the fact that I was merely killing time, to concentrate properly on the river. I believe rivers and fish know such things — they detect a fake. Besides, I had never heard of the Popo Agie until an hour before, and I am skeptical of rivers until they prove themselves to me. I fished by form rather than with passion, hopeful but not avid. The real fishing hadn't begun, I told myself. Nellie wandered back and forth, exploring the sage and meadow grasses. It was good to have her out. She splashed quite a bit but I didn't blame her.

In two hours' fishing I did not have a nibble. The sun began to run on the water, taking an angle and tucking shadows next to rocks and into the ripples. Crickets whirled in the light and landed on the water, riding the current, passing from sun to shadow. I watched to see if a trout took them, but the crickets rode out of sight, bobbing downstream, impervious, eventually tricks of light and distance transforming them to water. I changed flies regularly, trying to match the insects, but never unlocked the river.

Around five I called Nellie and we went back to the truck. While I pulled off my waders, she had a good roll in the dust. We drove into town with the windows halfway up, cold slipping down from the mountains. I parked next to The Good Place, the rendezvous spot with Bob and Tom, and waited.

The Wind River Range stretched all around us. I had been in the Winds before and knew some of their history. Though not as famous as the Grand Tetons, they are probably the greatest mountain range in Wyoming and arguably in the lower forty-eight states. The seven largest glaciers in the Rocky Mountain states are located in the Winds. Gannett Peak, at 13,804 feet, spikes the center of the range and is the highest peak in Wyoming. The Winds are granitic and separate the Green River basin to the south and west from the Wind River basin to the north and east. The range runs on a north-west diagonal along Route 287 from Atlantic City at the south end, up past Lander, Ft. Washakie, Crowheart, Burris, Dubois, eventually bleeding into the Grand Tetons at Moran Junction. On the southern rim, traveling Routes 189 and 191, you can hit Hoback Junction, Bondurant, and Pinedale. The range encompasses Shoshone National Forest, the Fitzpatrick Wilderness, Bridger National Forest, Bridger Wilderness, the Popo Agie Wilderness, and the Wind River Indian Reservation.

What we now call Wyoming is the land of Arapaho, Bannock, Blackfoot, Cheyenne, Crow, Sioux, Lakota, Ute, and Shoshone people. When French trappers began making their way down the rivers, sometime in the mid-1700s, the Indians were waiting for them, alerted by word of mouth. The Shoshone, who inhabited much of the Wind River area, were known as the "snake" Indians. They formed compact, isolated family groups, who collected seeds, roots, fish, birds, and small game such as rabbits in their proper season. They returned to the same areas once each year and referred to each other according to the main food source of a region. There were Seed Eaters, Rabbit Eaters, and so forth. If the family units had an abundance of food, they gathered together where winter was mild to form a village. After the Shoshone acquired horses from the Spaniards, they became buffalo hunters like the Plains tribes.

Sacagewea, who served as a guide and interpreter for Lewis and Clark, was a Shoshone. So were the chieftains Pocatello and Washakie. The Wind River Indian Reservation was presented to Chief Washakie in 1868 in return, our government said, for the Shoshone's friendliness to white people and their help in fighting tribes hostile to settlers. Washakie was buried in the town named after him, located halfway up the Winds. And it was near Ft. Washakie, just past the Wind River Indian Reservation, that Nellie and I were going to fish.

From inside the pickup we waited and watched the sun fade to a tired red, the long boulevard behind us growing shadowy and washed. Nellie nosed at a fly that had made its way to the dashboard. I reached into the truck bed and grabbed the green L.L. Bean dog pack I had already loaded with mittens and hats and her supply of dog food. I anchored it across her back by tightening the straps under her legs and across her chest. She sniffed at the pack, recognized it as hers, then looked straight ahead. *Hiking,* I told her, but she didn't seem to make much of that so I changed it to *Walk.* Immediately she perked up and stood, ready to go. I grabbed her front paws and made her dance the cha-cha a little. I put her ears above her head and told her she looked like a Russian peasant woman. She tolerated everything, although clearly she would have preferred a walk. The bear bells on her backpack tinkled whenever she moved.

THE 3: WINDS

AT TEN THOUSAND FEET in the Wind River Range of Wyoming, I caught the first trout of the trip. Bob and I had been casting in Dutch Oven Lake for nearly an hour, our lines sinking in water so clear that you could watch the fly drift to the bottom thirty or forty feet below. We had caught nothing, though occasionally small ducks—buffleheads, I thought, known locally as Spirit Ducks—flittered on the surface at the liquid slap of our five-weight lines. It was three o'clock and late September and the temperature was dropping again. Tom snapped photographs of us and lolled around, watching to see what kind of fishermen we might be. Nellie stood next to me, her chin against my left knee, her eyes waiting for the tiny explosion that meant trout.

"We should try the feeder streams," one of us said. It didn't matter which one of us said it. We both understood that the lake fishing was futile.

But we didn't move at first. We were all tired. We had hiked seven or eight miles that day with sixty-pound packs, gaining and losing then gaining again approximately three thousand feet along Bears Ears. We had already set up camp, gathered wood, and staked out our Eureka tent. The night before, in the high winds, the tent fly had torn free and flapped most of the night. None of us had slept well. Now, as the sun fell and pushed the temperature closer and closer to forty, it was tempting to give up on the fishing and head to our camp. To move at that altitude meant shortness of breath and a rapid heart and there was no guarantee that we would catch fish after hiking even farther.

I also think we suffered from a shared willingness to keep fishing no matter how unpromising the water. In fact, as odd as it might sound, I am suspicious that we frequently preferred not to catch fish. I have never talked to another fisherman about it, but after twenty years of fly-fishing I am almost certain most fishermen possess a peculiar bend to their makeup. Fishermen are optimists, and the fish in the future is always preferable to the fish at hand. Even the best fishermen catch fish only a small percentage of the time, which means we persevere in a sport that features failure as its main ingredient. Truly great days, when the fish hammer the fly as soon as it settles on the surface, are rare. They are especially rare in the East, unless one happens to be on a river or lake when the stocking truck delivers. Bob, I knew, was particularly prone to this low-grade masochism. One day on the Deerfield River in Massachusetts we arrived at dawn on a spring morning to find the dam-controlled waters gushing at an incredible height. Given the water conditions, we needed to be on the other bank, and after some debate we settled on a five-mile walk back to a bridge that traversed the river, then back up along the other side of the stream. It took hours, but when we finally arrived on the distant side the fishing was rewarding. We caught six or seven fourteen-inch rainbow trout within an hour. Bob, however, after two or three fish, became itchy. He knew he could catch fish there, he said, so what was the challenge? When I pointed out that we had walked five miles to get in position, and that, furthermore, we had been skunked at the Deerfield plenty of times, he was unmoved. He said he knew we could catch fish where we were, so what was the thrill?

It's a puzzling perspective to take for people who spend a considerable amount of time pursuing trout, but I've seen it manifest itself in enough fishing companions to know it's a part of the fishing equation. Perhaps it's as the wonderful fisherman-writer Roderick Haig-Brown said: "I want fish from fishing, but I want a great deal more than that and getting it is not always dependent on catching fish."

Eventually we moved from Dutch Oven. We had come several thousand miles, after all, and to stop at this point would have been disappointing, to say the least. Nellie led us along the shore until we came to the small stream spilling away from the lake. The stream had no name on our topo. It was a thin blue line snaking away from Dutch Oven, winding into willow bogs somewhere in the next valley. I told Nellie to sit, that we were going to fish, but she ignored me. She splashed into the first pool and drank for the time it took me to switch from a Blue Winged Olive to a black Letort's Cricket. It's common fishing wisdom to go to terrestrials in autumn, and the Letort replicated the small black grasshoppers that skittered the grass along the lake.

I cast to the tail of the pool, not far from where a log lay submerged beneath a white sheen of running water. In the instant the cricket landed, the white sheen seemed to gather its molecules and become a trout. The shape appeared not from the bottom or from the darkness near the log, but came, as a thought, to take the fly. I lifted the tip of my fly rod and suddenly the fish swirled and became separate from the water, and I saw it as an animal, a creature, and I led it to me. Nellie took a step into the water and watched, head cocked, to determine that this was not a stick to fetch. She looked back and forth from me to the fish. I told her to leave it, and she did, her ears tucked forward to listen, her fur dripping a drizzle into the cold stream.

It was a cutthroat, seven or eight inches long. I released it underwater and saw it flash back to its hiding spot, light breaking it apart and obscuring it. Nellie took another step forward, unsure of what had occurred. "Trout," I told her. After studying the word for a moment, she put her tongue in the water and lapped at it. Her fur, where the water touched it, blended from golden to mahogany.

"Got one," I told Bob when I walked downstream to join him a few minutes later. He stood next to a beautiful pool, fiddling with his line. Water slipped through three or four rocks near his boots, then blossomed into a wide pool perhaps five feet deep. Tom sat well back, his camera out and clicking. Nellie went to sit with Tom.

"What did you get it on?" Bob asked.

"A Letort's Cricket," I said. "Black."

"Okay," he said.

I sat and watched. It took Bob a few minutes to thread the leader through his cricket. We are both forty-four and our eyes aren't as quick as they used to be. "The shrinking world," Bob said under his breath, a common refrain these days for him. Then he had the fly ready and he waved the rod back and forth, doing a crossover cast to get his fly into the water. Immediately a trout rose and hooked itself. Bob looked at me and wiggled his hips a little in our infamous trout dance. It's an inelegant dance, usually reserved to taunt the other guy that he is one fish behind. This time, I think, it meant that we were at ten thousand feet in Wyoming and we had an entire stream of fish ahead of us.

When he brought it to hand, he said, "Cutthroat."

"How big?" Tom asked.

"Now?" Bob asked. "Or when we talk about it later?"

"Seven inches," I said. "Looks to be about an inch smaller than the one I caught."

Bob caught three cutthroat out of the pool before we moved downstream. Willows covered the riffles in some places, but in flat sections, when the water rose from the hummocks and cut banks to produce a glassy plain, we found trout. We fished for an hour and caught a dozen fish. Each one was a cutthroat and each one was seven to eight inches long. Red gashes marked their throats. If we were incautious and stepped too hard near the cut banks, the trout scattered like sugar on a tile floor. But in good moments the trout were willing and they charged our flies with the greediness of wild fish, the greediness of trout in small streams who must decide quickly and act accordingly. We stayed with the Letort's Cricket, seeing no reason to change.

We fished until the light became dull and flat and the temperature pressed close to freezing. My hands no longer listened to my instructions, or if they did, they did so grudgingly. Without direct sunlight, it was difficult to spot the fish at the bottom of the pools. Water became opaque. It was hard to keep track of the cricket, because the light turned the air into something like water, translucent and white. John Steinbeck called the evening hour before true sunset "the hour of the pearl," and he might have been addressing fishermen. Light pulled us away and the water seemed to close back over the trout.

Back at camp, with a fire going and a tin cup of Wild Turkey in hand, we made instant spaghetti with zucchini. Then we had hot chocolate and more bourbon and ate gorp. We talked about bears and about work and dragged out the topo maps so we could see where to fish the next day. We decided to hike to Valentine, the largest lake in the area, which had feeder streams dripping away to join with Little Valentine. When I stood to get more wood, I noticed our tents glimmered with frost, the V of their sides white silver, like geese wings bent on flight.

I gave Nellie a biscuit or two and combed her while we sat beside the fire. She was pooped. She had acquired the lazy, quiet state that I love so much in Goldens. Everything about her was soft and sleepy. She grunted happily when I brushed her. I checked her paws and legs. They appeared sound. Then I combed her tail and the feathering at the back of her legs. She didn't like that as much, but she endured it. I whispered into her ears that she was a mountain climber, a pack carrier, a squirrel chaser. She stayed next to me and curled beside the fire. Her fur took on heat and she began to snore.

It was late, close to bedtime, when coyotes began howling. The sound lifted off the peaks and swirled, making it impossible to determine where the yelps originated. Nellie climbed to her feet immediately, a long, warm growl rising in her throat. She moved over to me, the hair on her neck raised. At home, in the White Mountains, Nellie had come awake one night to the sound of coyotes in our back yard. They had arrived in the darkest hour, tearing suet out of the bird feeder, then yowling in a demented, terrible cry that made Nellie nearly insane with worry or desire to join them. This moment was different. The coyotes cried from up in the hills surrounding our fire, their voices blending, then cracking apart. I pulled Nellie closer. Coyotes can run a domestic dog to death, I knew, leading them away until the dog is exhausted. Then the coyotes circle and kill the dog, betraying the cousin-heart of whatever made the dog follow. But these coyotes were not close enough to be a threat. I made Nellie sit between my legs, then closed my arms around her chest. Her lungs vibrated with her growls and her eyes flashed in the firelight. I whispered into her ear and asked what the coyotes wanted. I asked her if she liked hearing the coyotes. I told her when she got older, when she couldn't go much beyond our New Hampshire dooryard, that she could remember these coyotes on this night in September. This was why we had come, I told her. This was a small payment on the debt I owed her.

By the time we reached Valentine Lake the next morning, it had already begun to hail. The hailstones made sizzling sounds as they came through the pines. Bob said he'd fish down, I'd fish up, which meant he'd go downstream and look for pools while I worked in from the headwaters. Before he left we had to take shelter under some pines to wait out the hardest spill of hail yet. Lightning whacked at the hills to the east. The sun stirred the clouds but didn't break through. It was going to be a long gray day. The temperature, according to Tom's thermometer, read forty-three degrees.

Tom went with Bob. Nellie came with me and we fished the shallows where the lake squeezed closed and tightened into the stream. I fished with the Letort's Cricket again, but after working several promising riffles, I switched to a Blue Winged Olive, then a Muddler Minnow, then a small Royal Coachman. Nothing. Nellie followed me from rock to rock, sometimes standing in the water, sometimes squeezing onto a perch with me. She was smart enough to stay to my left, well away from my back cast. I talked to her and told her what I was doing every time I changed position or switched flies. When I finally gave up and went to find Bob and Tom, she darted ahead and led me directly to them.

Bob was having better luck. He had worked his way down to a waterfall about a half mile downstream. He had already caught four or five, he said, right out of the white water below the falls. I told him I had struck out and he did a small trout dance, but not the full blown version to torture me.

The hail began again. It had been coming on and off, pecking the water for five minutes at a time, then ceasing without any appreciable change in the clouds overhead. This time, though, the hail drove us under the pines again. For a while we didn't say anything. Bad weather is death to camping trips, we knew. We didn't relish the notion of sitting in a tent and playing cards the rest of the day. We were also aware that we were approximately eleven miles away from the trailhead and that to reach any source of heat besides the fire we might make, we would have to climb a pass that took us above twelve thousand feet. It was possible, Tom pointed out, that the hail could turn to snow and we would be in a tricky spot. So we stood sedately as cows beneath the trees, our collars up, the hail pelting off us after it struck. The forest floor became covered in white patches. The hail resembled rock salt, the bony crystals one spreads on an icy sidewalk. It was a hailstorm as a child might draw a hailstorm.

"I'm not eating you," Bob told me after a time, "no matter how hungry I get."

"We should get over the pass, at least," Tom said. "Before this gets worse."

We kicked it around a little. Our original plan had been to spend the entire day fishing the feeder streams, then hike either to the Continental Divide or halfway out the next morning. The day after that, we intended to push through to the trailhead where Bob and Tom would head to Salt Lake City for their return flights, and Nellie and I would continue on the lazy U that connected to the gradual return route through Montana. We had a month or more; Bob and Tom had only two days.

"Your call," I told them. "But we can fish some nice places along Route 287 in the next day and a half. We could make it to Lander tonight, then Dubois tomorrow."

"I vote for a warm motel room," Tom said.

We decided to make a run for it, which meant we had to hike eleven miles before sunset. To make it more difficult, we were getting a late start. But we were confident that we could bivouac if we had to, bedding down against a rock formation if necessary. If we stayed, it would be cold and miserable sleeping at best, while movement, we thought, would be better than remaining stationary. It was worth a try, we concluded, even if we only made it halfway out.

My main concern was Nellie. She had hiked well on the way in, carrying her food and biscuits in the green dog pack, but she was eleven, after all. She was willing, certainly, and that was my chief worry. I didn't doubt that she would stay with us, but I wondered at what cost. She had no way to inform us that she was tired or cold. I also knew, from experience, that her feet attracted ice and snow to the hairy webs between her toes.

51

During our snowshoeing in winter, she stopped constantly to bite ice from her feet, at times moving only a few yards before repeating the process. The hail had a different consistency from snow, but I wondered if it would plague her, making our progress slower than necessary. Not for the first time, I calculated her age in human terms. The old adage that one human year is equal to seven dog years has been revised by most owners. The current thinking is that a dog year is equal to seven human years for the first three or four years of a dog's life and four years thereafter. Using that formula, Nellie was a little older than me, in her early fifties. I thought she'd make it fine, though I determined to watch her closely.

We packed. The hail stopped for a time, then started again. My clothes and boots were already wet. The pack felt heavy on my shoulders, which were stiff from carrying it the last two days. Nellie must have felt the same thing, because when I approached her with her dog pack, she shied from it. After cajoling and calling her closer, I finally snapped it on and we started off a little before noon. Nellie led the way. The hail came and went, came and went, without any appreciable change in the temperature or cloud patterns. We started up, mounting the switchbacks that would take us to the pass at twelve thousand feet. When it hit the back of my legs, the hail stung. It stung more than I could anticipate, so that each time it came it surprised me with its urgency. It wanted to be through me. It wanted to pass my skin and fall on the ground.

It was a dull climb. The hail kept us pinned to the side of the mountain and more than once we huddled together, our backs turned into the wind. Now and then I met Bob's eye. This was our bad gris-gris once again. As boys we had almost drowned off the New Jersey coast, each of us clinging to a jetty rope in waves far too rough, both of us surviving by miracles of stupidity, and now here we were again. He shook his head at me and told me it was my fault. I told him he was the source of our bad luck. And the wind kept rising in velocity, driving the hail sideways against us.

Nellie, fortunately, climbed without difficulty. The hail was too wet to cling to her feet. She splashed ahead, apparently untroubled. That much was a relief. We worried, however, that the trail would be lost in the snow, so we could not take our allotted rest, but had to continue climbing, pushing ourselves to clear the pass. For at least two miles the world consisted entirely of my wet boots, mosquito swarms of snow, and the dense rocks and lichen that marked our way.

It took three hours to reach the pass. We stood for a moment at the highest point of our travel. A glint of sun came out and the hail subsided for a moment. Then, quicker than we could take it in, the sun disappeared again and the hail started once more. The wind, though, had quartered and now pressed on our backs. It made me think that the mountain had finished with us. We walked single file, Nellie leading. She doubled back whenever she couldn't see me, checking to make sure I was still with her. If I stopped, even in this storm, I understood she would stay with me. She wouldn't be happy, and she would think we could do better than a spot in a hailstorm, but she would stay nonetheless. Even if I wanted to, I could not send her away.

My first fishing trip took place on Mindowaskin Pond in the center of Westfield, New Jersey. Westfield is a moderate-sized bedroom community of approximately thirty-five thousand people, located thirty miles due west of New York City. It was not anything approaching a wilderness. Nevertheless, Mindowaskin Pond had its charms. The Protestant church, a wedding-white building sitting on the highest hill in town, overlooked the water in a pleasing way. The church laid out a nativity scene each December on a small island in the center of the pond. Beyond the island, close to the southernmost end of the pond, stood a small footbridge made of fieldstone. On skating nights, at least as I remember them, the boys and girls congregated on the bridge in order to push one another and steal hats, their fleeing and pursuing accomplished in thumping runs before the slap onto ice and glinting glide. A bandstand sprouted near the bridge, a wide, clumsy affair, where each December the Lions or Elks put on a community wassail, the men's voices ruddy in the cold, their scarves bright and festive, their long, houndstooth overcoats as respectable as wood.

My first real experience with Mindowaskin Pond, and with fishing, occurred sometime in August of my ninth or tenth year. It had been a listless summer. Both of my intimate friends, Bobby Mullen who lived behind me, and Frank Reynolds who lived up the street, were away at camp. I had spent most of the summer reading the Hardy Boys, their delicious brown jacket covers leaving a taste of themselves on my finger each time I wet it to turn a page. Curled in a chair on our screened-in porch, I had already read *Kon Tiki, Call of the Wild, The Leatherstocking Tales, Tom Swift and His Magic Submarine, The Kid Who Batted 1,000,* and *Robinson Crusoe.* Naturally after devouring a diet of such books, I was ripe for adventure. Although camp was a rather exotic notion to me, I desperately wanted to attend. According to Bobby and Frank, campers' days consisted of paddling around in birchbark canoes, shooting arrows at targets shaped like deer, and winging rocks at the turtles that came to sun on the logs of old Camp Kikitah. I yearned to be a *little brave*, the name given to newcomers. I determined that I would be the finest camper imaginable, perhaps even earning an Indian name in a secret ceremony run, again according to Bobby and Frank, by a full-blooded Iroquois named Mr. Brownfeather.

It did not occur to me to bring up the question of camp with my mother or father. I was the last of seven children, a final boy born when my mother was forty-two years old, so at the time of my first expedition to Mindowaskin Pond, she must have been over fifty. In our family we did not discuss frills, though we were far from being poor. My father was a corporate executive who commuted each day to New York City. Nevertheless, we seldom had money for extras, and it was understood, if not expressed, that one did not ask frivolously for items not covered under the ongoing budget. Even at the age of nine or ten I understood this sort of large-family spartanism.

Still, there was the matter of camp. I'm certain, in my way, I let it be known that I was enduring a disappointing summer. I have no other way to explain why my mother sought me out early one summer day on the porch with a copy of our local paper, *The Westfield Leader*, in her hand.

"Did you see this, honey?" she asked me. "Right there, under the ad?"

It was an announcement for a fishing derby, an open invitation to children around town to come fish Mindowaskin Pond. A benevolent organization, perhaps the Elks or Lions, had stocked the pond with goldfish. Three of the fish, the ad stated, were not gold but silver instead. These silver fish were redeemable for ten dollars at the Playfair, our local toy store. In order to be eligible to fish, one had to be under thirteen years of age and a resident of the town.

I wish I could say that I embraced the situation, that I agreed with my mother that this was just the opportunity for which I had been waiting, but I was aware this was a half prize: it was something offered when the better, truer thing is out of one's reach. Like most children growing up in a large family, I had experienced it before. I had worn my sister's white skates rather than the pair of hockey skates I coveted. I had asked for a yellow slicker to wear in the rain and had received, instead, a yellow rubber parka, the flappy, plastic kind one sometimes carries in a backpack to use in an emergency as a tent or ground cloth. The fish derby, I suspected, was a deal struck along those same lines.

But as I had nothing else to do that day, and because my mother offered the outing to me in good faith, I accepted. One problem existed: I had no fishing pole. My mother, however, had even anticipated that objection. Years ago, when my grandfather had maintained a small house on the Chesapeake Bay, our family had acquired four or five deep-water poles. I knew of the poles' existence. They had remained in the southeast corner of our basement for at least a decade. I had examined them any number of times, but had always stopped short of ever trying to use them because they were "damn good rods" according to the family myth.

But this, remarkably, was what my mother proposed. I was to take whichever rod I liked, rig it up, and use it to win the prize goldfish down at Mindowaskin Pond.

It was an extraordinary plan. Soon I was seated in our enormous Buick 225, a bag of peanut butter and jelly sandwiches on the floor beside me, a rigid black pole extending from the front seat to the space beneath the back window. For hooks, I had a package of my mother's safety pins. For bait, I had the bread of my peanut butter and jelly sandwiches and a few hunks of bologna. The bologna was surefire bait, I felt. It would smell better to fish than worms, and it clung to the safety pins like fleshy barnacles. My mother dropped me near the bandstand. I sensed immediately that this was one of those events where it was handy to have a parent along, preferably a father, although I guessed there would be some well-intentioned men hanging around trying to help. My mother, I knew, would be of no use in this kind of enterprise. I told her I would be home at sunset— it was early morning, perhaps nine o'clock—and that there was no need to worry about me, I could swim for goodness sake. She kept the car idling while I slowly extracted my chosen fishing rod. I put it over my shoulder and headed to Mindowaskin Pond.

Anyone familiar with the impossibility of casting line from a deep-water pole, or of using pocket-warm bologna to bait a safety pin, has already anticipated what my day was like. Because I could not cast the line more than two or three feet from the edge of the pond, I was soon frustrated and angry. I blamed my parents for not sending me to camp. I blamed the town fathers for holding the event in the first place. I blamed my stupid safety pin hooks which were, I soon realized, large enough to yank the liver out of the tiny carp floating around the shimmering pond.

Time moved. A few boys I knew from school passed by sporting lightweight spinning rods and broke my heart with the ease with which they launched their casts. I wanted to ask their advice; I wanted to punch them. Mostly I wanted to hide the awkwardness of my ridiculous fishing pole, my absurd bait, my cumbersome twine leader.

Near noon I ate lunch sitting beneath an old maple. It was cool in the shade, a perfect day really. I ate two peanut butter and jelly sandwiches, gulped down the pint of lemonade my mother had included in my lunch, and finished everything off with a chocolate Devil Dog. I wanted to go home. I wanted to get away from the pond, although I could think of no way to return to my mother's questions without exploding in anger at her for putting me in such a humiliating situation. I hated her. I hated myself. I hated the largeness of my family which had turned so many simple pleasures into exercises in embarrassment.

Exhausted and gloomy, I fell asleep. I must have gone out deeply because I woke to find it late in the day, probably around four, the sun already softening. Enough time had passed to allow me to depart, and I was tremendously relieved. I stood and dusted myself off, then began gathering my things. I had almost finished when I realized the pond was nearly deserted. One or two boys still fished up near the small spillway at the north end, but otherwise the water was glassy and lonely.

For reasons I've never identified, I returned to the water, rigged up my pole once more, and spent the next three hours entirely lost. The light had changed. Sunlight no longer reflected so obliquely off the surface, so suddenly the underworld opened to my view. Now instead of casting blindly to fish I couldn't see, my hook suddenly rested in plain sight, the sluggish carp sucking their way past in endless hope and promise.

I didn't catch a fish, although once or twice I came close. One fish actually ate my bait which made me tremble inside my skin. I didn't lure a fish close again that day—and did not, in fact, catch a fish until a distant summer in the Poudre Valley

58

outside of Fort Collins, Colorado in my twenty-first year — but I had begun my apprenticeship.

That day marked me as a fisherman. Whatever it is that draws some people to water, and to fishing, bit me then and there. On that first trip I learned that it was possible to enter the water, to forget to search arriving cars to see if my mother had come to fetch me. I learned it is possible to lose all sense of time, to look up suddenly from a hatch or feeding frenzy and find oneself momentarily removed from solid earth. I go fishing not to find myself, I learned that day, but to lose myself.

WARM SPRINGS
4:

ON THE LAST FIFTY YARDS OF THE HIKE, Nellie chased a squirrel up a tree. Her movement remained bright and sharp despite our weariness at hiking eleven miles. She had chased squirrels throughout the long day, never coming close to catching one, but going, at times, alarmingly near to the drop-offs we crossed. The marmots at the higher elevations taunted her mercilessly, squeaking in a perverse circuit to keep her from zeroing in on one individual. The result was that she had probably covered two or three miles more than we had.

As I watched her in that last sprint, I worried again about what it would cost her to have walked so far in a day. Once, while hiking in the White Mountains of New Hampshire, we had hiked all day, bagging three 4,000 footers in a ten hour stretch. When we returned to my car, she lay next to the rear tires as I stripped off my backpack, hardly responsive when I called her to get inside. Eventually I tempted her with a biscuit, but as soon as she finished chewing, she fell asleep, her body twitching in exhaustion. The same thing, I was afraid, might happen this time. And now, of course, she was a good deal older than she had been.

But I worried about Tom, too. His knee had gone out, buckling on an old injury, the heavy backpack aggravating it at each step. He had kept on, not complaining, but he was done in. With two miles to go, Bob and I agreed that I should go ahead so that I could have my truck warmed and ready to move. It meant that I had to walk an extra quarter mile to the parking area, but that was all right. I felt surprisingly strong, my only problem a numbed left arm where my shoulder strap cut too sharply into my circulation.

Nellie, to my delight, climbed into the passenger side when we arrived at the truck and fell instantly asleep. She climbed in without difficulty. I woke her for a moment to give her a peanut butter cracker with a Bufferin secreted in the goop. She ate it in three quick chews, then put her chin back on the soft seat cushion. She did not bother me for more crackers. I thumbed the pads on her feet, checked her legs, and then let her rest.

Tom and Bob had gained the trailhead by the time I returned to them with the truck. When I pulled into the loop beside the brown trail sign, Tom's voice was wobbly with cold. We had been chilled down to the core, the snow and hail making every step wet. All of us steamed. The truck heater could not heat us down to where we were cold.

As we threw our packs in the truck—everything wet and dank smelling—Bob pulled out beers and passed them around. It was close to six o'clock. We had hiked approximately eight hours without a substantial rest. I couldn't speak for the others, but I felt the elation that always comes at the end of long physical days. I was conscious of my body—its workings, its aches and pains—in a way that my everyday life does not demand. The beer tasted good. The heat inside the truck cab, when I ducked inside to stack my equipment, was incredibly welcome. I liked knowing what we had done, how far we had hiked, what we had endured. I liked the memory of those trout living beneath the cut banks, their bodies quick and hidden.

The road off the mountain, and through the Wind River Indian Reservation, followed a series of long switchbacks, each one bringing us close to the edge of sheer drop-offs, only to catch us and make us hug the mountain again. The sun fell behind us and we could look out and see fifty, sixty, seventy miles of the Absoraka mountains. Cattle grazed on the side of the hills, and occasionally pronghorn antelope lifted their heads at our passing. I kept my hand on Nellie. She slept with her chin flat between her front paws, her eyes solidly shut. Once, when we were halfway to the bottom of the switchbacks, she made the half barking, half crying sound that she makes in deep sleep. *Get him,* I whispered to her, imagining, as I always did when I heard that sound, that she chased rabbits through open meadows, the pursuit more exciting than the catch could ever be.

Forty-five minutes later, we were back in Lander at a modest motel. A tall blonde woman who smelled sharply of cigarette smoke rented us two rooms for thirty-five dollars apiece. She said she had no problem at all with a dog staying in my room, a healthy attitude that I encountered throughout the West. I pulled my truck over to room fourteen and parked. Nellie did not stir when I turned off the engine, which was a bad sign. I went around the truck and opened the room door, set up the dog bed near a heating register, then came back for Nellie. As quick and curious as she is normally, she refused to budge when I called her to climb down. Her tail flicked once or twice in the manner that indicates she heard me, likes me plenty, but I can go to hell. In the end I had to lift her out of the truck, putting her gently onto her feet. I patted my thigh and got her to follow me into the motel room. She did not bother with the dog bed, but folded flat on the floor as soon as she crossed the threshold, ignoring food when I poured it out and the water that I put near her nose.

"You okay?" I asked her. I knelt next to her and patted her for a while. She didn't acknowledge my hand at all. I massaged her legs a little, kneading the muscles lightly with my fingers. After a while I stood and unpacked the truck, then took a long hot shower. When I checked on her again, she hadn't moved. She still did not respond to my hand. I was petting her when Bob and Tom arrived, ready to go out for hot food.

I was reluctant to leave Nellie, but I didn't know what I could do for her in her current state. We went in their rental car to a diner at the edge of town. Tom's knee was slightly improved. We sat in a booth and hardly talked. We were tired. We were also stunned to find ourselves out of the mountains and in a restaurant, a warm bed waiting down the road. We ate full dinners, slices of pie, and several cups of coffee. When we arrived back at the motel, Nellie still hadn't moved. After I said goodnight to Bob and Tom, I lifted her into bed. It wasn't easy. I had to kneel next to her, work my hands under her like the arms of a forklift, then hoist her slowly. She grunted a little as I lifted her, but she didn't move otherwise. I put her carefully on one side of the bed, covered her, then climbed in beside her. I was as exhausted as she, but I also felt the wonderful exhilaration of being in a clean, comfortable bed, feeling warm, knowing that I could get up and get a cup of water or use the bathroom — luxurious things after camping. When I finally became too tired to stay awake, I rolled over next to her and rubbed her belly. She wasn't too tired to lift a leg to give me better access to her stomach and I took that as a promising sign. I listened to her breathe for a time. Then I was out and didn't have another thought until morning.

When I woke after eight hours of sleep, Nellie hadn't changed position. I showered again and dressed, then attached Nellie's leash and coaxed her off the bed. She didn't like it much, but at least she was able to move. We walked slowly across the street to a weedy lot I had seen the night before. She did her business deliberately, then followed me back to the motel room. I tried to lift her with my voice, getting her to feel some excitement, but she wasn't buying. I forced her to eat another peanut butter cracker with a Bufferin, then shook her uneaten food in her bowl. She took two or three nibbles and I understood, just by the return of her appetite, that she would be okay.

By mid-morning Nellie was moving better. We drove to Dubois for lunch and spent an hour poking around town. While we had been in the mountains, the season had changed. Although there were still some fly fishermen along the Wind River, Dubois was given over to elk hunters. The wide streets were dotted with pickup trucks and campers, men in orange jackets standing beside them. Up in the mountains, as we well knew, snow had already come.

Bob and I visited the Orvis dealer in the center of town. I don't much like fly shops, feeling, as I do when I enter them, the pressure of commercialization. Twenty years ago, when I began fly fishing, I bought a pair of Red Ball plastic waders, a twenty dollar fly rod, and a package of flies from a local sporting goods store. It never occurred to me that I wasn't properly outfitted. Now the sport is filled with anglers who fly to Montana for the weekend, spend hundreds of dollars on fancy waders and wading sticks, buy fly jackets with emergency inflatable collars, and fork out three to four hundred dollars a day for float trips. I suppose many of these men are fine anglers—and on the streams they are quick to tell you about hatches, water temperatures, emergers, and spinner returns—but something is inevitably lost in such elaborate packaging. It seems a particularly American failing to take a sport that is ideally about quietude and symmetry and turn it into a marketing campaign. I don't want a lamp shaped like a trout; I don't want a trash can with a picture of a trout rising to a fly on the side; I don't want a trout phone. As a result, I do most of my fly gear shopping at a local hardware store where I can pick out leaders that are hung next to red and white bobbers, hooks next to barbecue forks.

But the clerk at the Orvis store—a southerner from the Carolinas who moved west after trout—was helpful and low-key. Because Bob and Tom had to leave by five that afternoon, we inquired if there was a river or stream nearby that might entertain us for the afternoon. The clerk didn't hesitate. He directed us to Warm Springs, a stream a few miles outside of town. He told us that it was fine dry-fly fishing, that we could wade it easily, and that we should fish up from the bridge that crossed the water. I decided that if it was suitable, I'd camp there for the night. The Orvis clerk told us to be mindful of bears. As all people who live in the West seem to delight in telling bear stories, particularly to people from back East, we listened to the usual litany of bear sightings, confrontations, pepper spray encounters, and reports of bear activity. We said we'd keep an eye out. Then we headed up into the mountains, driving this time instead of walking, the sun at our backs.

Most anglers, just before sleep, cast to remembered trout on remembered summer days, reading water as it breaks over sandbars, wading in sunlight, a hatch of mayflies sugaring the water just upstream. Hemingway, perhaps, wrote first about the practice, but I'm sure it is a habit as old as fishing itself. Lying awake just short of sleep, I cast to fish on the Wood River in Rhode Island, the Deerfield in Massachusetts, Hall Pond in New Hampshire, and a nameless pond I once fished in Canada, one where a shoreline of young salmon took my March Brown fly on every cast and a bald eagle halved a summer moon when I happened to glance up. I think, too, of Burkina Faso, West Africa, when as a young Peace Corps volunteer I went to the tsetse-covered Black Volta River and fished for electric catfish, catching them in water still and black. Near sunset a python dropped out of a tree and landed in the water next to me, its meated body touching mine for an instant before it decided, for reasons I've never understood, to swim across the river away from me. I remember that.

The bridge to which the Orvis clerk had directed us spanned a steam approximately thirty yards wide. It is a stream I will remember for some time. A level gravel parking spot spread beneath the bridge, and I backed in close to the river, so that, in sleeping, I would hear the rush of water over rocks. When I opened the door for Nellie, she hopped out immediately, her legs good, her movement vastly improved. She waded into the stream and took a long drink. Tom decided to stay with the vehicles. His knee still hurt and, besides, he had no interest in fishing. I gave him a folding camp chair to use, then went with Bob upstream, both of us using black Letort's Crickets again. The stream bent under the bridge and flattened, and I imagined, as I often do when I begin fishing, that the river had no bed, that the fish inhabited a seam in the earth. Bob said for me to go upstream a few hundred yards, that he would fish the bottom ripples, and that we would rendezvous in about an hour. I agreed and headed off. Nellie went with me, her tail up, her chest crashing through brush and the tall grasses that lined the water.

Fifty yards away, I stopped at a pool that arced in a half moon to my right, noon to three o'clock. Water chiggered over rocks, flooding in white arrows down toward a deep wedge that settled against the far bank. I watched the water for a while and made certain that Nellie didn't clump into the pool. The sun fell hard on my back, the heat sufficient so that the water splashing onto the flat rocks at the edge of the stream dried before it could stain the rocks dark. It was about three o'clock.

I made sure I had enough slack in my line before attempting the first cast. I did three quick back casts, then let the fly settle on the surface of the water. A trout rose immediately. I saw its body flash through the water first, the glint of something moving, then it grabbed the fly and soared clear of the water. It was a seven-inch cutthroat, light but urgent, and I led it easily to the slack water at my feet. When released, the trout shot through water that seemed too shallow to accommodate it. I waited a moment before casting again, letting my heart slow.

It took five casts to catch another trout. Another five to catch another trout. Each time the fly landed on the water, I saw the glimmer of trout rising to inspect it. It reminded me that trout do not truly swim toward a fly, but instead cock their lateral fins and soar upward on the force of the approaching water, like children, arms out, pretending to fly into the wind. In moving water a trout rise is not the product of rhythmic strokes, but a dive into air.

Some time later Bob passed behind me. He said he had caught a few below and was going to leapfrog me, heading up above to try his luck there. Nellie trailed after him. I told him I'd catch up with him in a few minutes. The pool in front of me continued to be productive, although it slowed until I had to cast fifteen or twenty times before I had a strike. Still, I have spent days casting in the East without a single hit and I was happy to run the fly over the pool. I came to know one particular dip in the water where the trout apparently clustered. I changed flies twice, opting finally for an auburn dry fly I had tied myself. I caught three fish on it, proving that trout cannot distinguish a well-made fly from one of my homely efforts. Water sounds covered me, and it was not until I moved away from the stream, taking a path through the grasses to join Bob, that I realized the sound of my thinking and the sound of running water had combined for more than an hour without my detecting it.

I found Bob standing at a bend in the river, Nellie beside him, his attention focused on tying a new fly onto his leader.

"Two up under that bank," Bob said when I approached, his chin pointing upstream, "and then I lost my fly."

We poked around for a while. The water slid against the rocks in just the right way. I changed flies once or twice, but it was more to stop and think about things than any sort of response to the river. I liked being on the river with Bob. Watching him, I could frequently see the boy that he had been glimmering just on the edge of his movement. It made me glad to know that boy was still around.

We fished downstream and I caught nothing until I arrived at the first place I had tried. Immediately I tied into three fish. I've often wondered about the luck of a specific pool, whether it is simply that water is rich with fish in one location, or whether, catching something, we become better anglers because our casts count for something. Either way, the fish cooperated. The sun, however, had started to settle on the shoulders of the mountains and the water began to smoke with the first evening chill. Bob fished the pool near the bridge again, but didn't catch anything. I was reminded that we never know which fish might be our last. I tried to make that into a large, philosophical finding, but I was too lazy and tired from all the hiking.

We walked back to the truck and found Tom reading a book, content to sit by the river on such a fine afternoon. But the cold had found him, too, and he had pulled on a jacket. We all talked for a while, then Bob said it was time to get going. It took only a minute for them to pack and get ready to leave.

I told Bob that we would do some ice fishing in the winter. He agreed. I shook Tom's hand and said it was good to meet him. Then they took off, at five, disappearing over the hump in the road that led down to Dubois and then on to Jackson Hole. I heard their engine for a while until the water behind me swallowed it and I was alone.

I made oatmeal with maple syrup on my cookstove while the temperature dropped and numbed my hands. I ate sitting on the camp chair beside the water, Nellie scouting around, but I knew it would be an early night. For a while after dinner I did nothing at all. I sat in the chair and listened to the water, felt the cold fall out of the mountains and surround me. Nellie returned from her exploration and butted me with her head until I let her lay her chin on my lap for a long pet. We stayed like that for a time. Later I got up and washed the oatmeal away in the stream, scrubbed the spoons and cups, brushed my teeth. For a moment I squatted next to the stream, a man panning for gold, my hands and wrists red with cold.

Not later than seven, I climbed into the back of the truck. It was too cold to stay in the open air. I closed the back and slithered into my sleeping bag, kicking my legs a little to get warm. Ice began to form on the inside windows of the truck. I fell asleep immediately, but woke, at two, to Nellie's shivers. I unzipped the sleeping bag and let her climb inside, awkwardly wrapping it around us both. She lay next to me, her chin on my gut, her shivers pulling us awake to the noise of the river—this one, or a thousand like it—sliding past rock.

At our house on Port Hood Island, Nova Scotia, lobsters lived in the shallows off the beach. It was illegal to take lobsters in pots unless one was properly licensed, but catching them by hand was dubious local custom. It had turned into a game for Nellie and me and after working in the fish shed most mornings, we ate a quick lunch and headed off on safari, a trout net our only weapon.

We kept a trim lawn for perhaps an acre around the house, but that acre quickly gave way to luxurious tall grasses, waist high at least, through which I had cut a sickled path. Nellie loved fishing for lobsters. As soon as she saw me grab the flippers she shot off down the meadow path, her tail a white puff retreating through the grass. By the time I strapped on my flippers and adjusted my mask and snorkel, she had already climbed onto the barnacled rocks that lined our beach, her eyes

impatiently scanning the surface. Minutes later, when I flattened onto the water, my flippers twitching me forward, she
crashed into the water beside me. Some days she carried a
tennis ball in her mouth, but most days she simply paddled for
the sake of paddling, her breathy *chaaa chaaa chaaaa* the motor
of our enterprise.

Once we settled in the water, I hooked a hand on her collar
and let my weight dangle in the smooth swells. The water
quickly deepened, dropping off to twenty or thirty feet in no
time at all. Clinging to her and paddling with my feet, I let her
guide me around the small bay, my eyes locked to the kelp beds
below. Lobsters are not easy to spot. They are not red, of course,
until you cook them, so their black backs blend with the ocean
bottom. Not until they venture into the small squares of sand
that connect the kelp beds are they readily visible. Moreover,
the water refracts their outline, making them appear small and
inconsequential. They might be an insect, or a dot of grass, and
it is not until you dive below, the water a rubbery pressure, that
you know what you have.

In August during our second year on the island, Nellie
learned to dive after me. We had experienced a string of warm
afternoons, the heat rising out of the ground. Our excursion was
tied to the tides, because I found it easier to hunt lobster when
the water receded and the rocky shore arched its back into the
sun. A bald eagle at the far end of the island accompanied us, its
flight out to a distant breakwater hectored by starlings and
crows. I spotted the first lobster about twenty feet from the
beach. Taking a deep breath, I did a frog dive, angling at forty-
five degrees to the square of sand where I had seen the lobster.
As soon as it spotted me, it began the oddly mechanical retreat
I counted on. Backing and lifting its pincers like the blade of a

72

bulldozer, it waited for me to advance. I knew what to do. I waved one hand at it to get its attention while I scooped behind it with the trout net. It backed into the net and I hoisted it, my lungs starting to ask for oxygen, my body chilled in the white current at the bottom of the sea. Usually I would push up from the ocean floor and swim toward air as rapidly as possible. This time, however, I chanced to look up and saw Nellie swimming through the ocean above me, no longer a creature flattened on the surface, but instead an ursine presence, a polar bear threading through water toward me. She could not go deep. I doubted her back was beneath the surface by more than a foot or two, but the sun stood as a disk behind her and she was under the sea, bars of light connecting us. The entire episode lasted only an instant. It seemed, though, that she floated in air, her paws boxing the dull gray of the sea water. In the silence from below I saw her fur rising and falling with the motion of the water, saw her drifting away from me on the tide even as she tried to follow. Then it was finished and I shot up to the surface, the lobster a rocky weight in the trout net.

It was a perspective I had never had before. We lolled in the surf, playing at the diving game. Her body fat kept her afloat, but I found she could sustain a bobbing sort of bear dive, a leisurely wallow through the easy summer swells. She knew how to hold her breath.

I hadn't thought of the diving game in years, but at a deep pool a mile from the campground, I remembered it. I stopped at the pool for lunch, feeling contented and rested. I felt the hike down in my bones. I let Nellie explore. She turned over sticks and sniffed one area, at the base of a tree, for an inordinate amount of time. Something had doubtless marked it with scent. She turned one shoulder to it eventually and rolled to take on the odor. I told her to leave it alone, that I had no desire to sleep in the back of the truck with a smelly dog. She ignored me. I sat for a while on the shoreline, astonished, as always, at the joy she took in discovering a new, fetid smell, then stood and went to the water.

I had no intention of swimming, but I wanted her to swim. Wearing Tevas, I waded in and found the water numbing. Nellie splashed in beside me, her tail and rump flattening on the water in a beaver silhouette. She made a small circuit of the watering hole, then came back and shook water all over me. I bent and sniffed near her. She smelled horrible. The water, only half applied, made the odor worse. Cursing a little under my breath, I decided to wash her. I stripped off my clothes and dove in, the cold whacking me.

The pool wasn't large, but it was deep. My breath huffed in my lungs. Cold, I kept thinking, until I moved enough to be, if not warm, at least momentarily comfortable. Nellie stayed with me. *Chaaa, chaaa, chaaa* her breath came. I grabbed her collar and let her pull me. I splashed water on her back, up on her head, everywhere I could reach. We were washing and swimming like that when I remembered the lobster game. It had been eight years at least since we had visited Port Hood Island, since the house overlooking the sea had been sold, since Amy and I had divorced. I dived down, pulling for the bottom, then tucked myself into a ball and looked up. The water was not particularly clear, but Nellie was there, tugging at the strings of light that passed through the surface, her body fighting its own buoyancy. For a moment neither of us advanced or retreated. She hung her head down, searching for me. Then I started for the surface and she went up for air.

The next day, I gave myself a lazy morning. As soon as the sun cleared the surrounding mountains, I moved my camp chair over to the light and sat with a large cutting board on my lap. The cutting board is my own invention, a kind of portable fly-tying bench. If I sit just the right way, I can clamp the cutting board between my knees and hook the vise to the left edge. The rest of the board provides a platform where I can lay out materials or put the finished fly when I am done. Because I am an atrocious flytier, it hardly matters that the setup is a bit rocky. I managed to churn out a few Hornbergs. The Hornberg is a multipurpose fly, replicating as it does a suggestion of caddis life and the weedy lives of minnows. I tied it because I am slow and because it gives me two flies, so to speak, for the price of one. I have always found it an effective scouting or attractor fly, one you can cast to empty water in the hope of finding where the trout might be hiding. I tied four of them before getting bored. Then I had a good time sitting with the board between my knees, winnowing out the used or rusted flies I had been carrying around for years.

I also tied together a new leader, which is my least favorite part of fishing. I am not particularly good at knots or understanding the calibrations of micrometers. I tie leaders in much the same way as I visit the dentist—because it is good for me once or twice a year. I also have little patience for the intricacies of tippet size, the thin, final connection between the fly and line. I have been on a river or pond too many times when I have caught twenty, thirty, even forty fish in a day. I am the same angler, I reason, when I catch nothing at all. My sense, after years of fishing, is that fish will bite if they're there. Proper tippet size is a help, certainly, but it is not the necessity many sporting journals make it out to be. Besides, there is an ongoing balance between equipment demands and actual fishing time. I prefer to toss it and let the trout decide to play or not. The advice I once heard attributed to a Scottish guide has always seemed correct to me. "Keep your eye on the fly," he is supposed to have said, "and your fly in the water." It's easy, in other words, to get caught in too much fussiness.

As I finished tying my leader, a camper pulled off the road and began backing into position twenty yards from my truck. I was disappointed to see it because I had hoped to spend a day or two sitting beside the river without any company besides Nellie. I saw at least two men in the front of the camper. A third jumped out of the side door and began giving the driver instructions, itching with his fingers to back a little more, a little more, there. I held Nellie's collar and waited to see how things developed.

They were elk hunters. The men popped out of the camper and waved to me. They all wore camouflage pants. The driver got busy setting jacks and making the camper level. The other two fellows began unloading. In no time they had coolers in a circle around them, folding chairs arranged, a small awning cranked out of the side of the camper. They had brought their back porch, in other words, and appeared immensely pleased that the comfort they expected at home could be transported to this remote spot in Wyoming. I felt crabby watching them. I knew I was being selfish, but I couldn't help it. Something inside the camper hummed. Maybe it was a heater, maybe it was a fan, but I wanted it off so that the sound of the water would remain unobscured.

76

Nellie strained to go visit, so I called over and asked if they minded if my dog came over. No, they said, no problem. I let Nellie go and she began shamelessly wagging her entire hindquarters before she had covered half the distance between us. I knew she was setting them up for future food begging, but they didn't know that. She was on her best behavior and went from one man to the next, happily stepping on their toes.

I decided I'd fish a while and see how things sorted themselves out. I pulled on my waders and slipped on my fly jacket. Nellie came back, ready to go. I waved to one of the hunters who had noticed my departure, but the other two had disappeared inside. I headed downstream. Nellie happily trotted with me.

Almost at once I came to a good pool where the water bent against the bank and deepened into a thick black. I tried my most recent Hornberg and caught a five-inch trout on my third cast. I did not take my success as an endorsement by the trout of my flytying. It was likely that the trout had been waiting, happy to skim up to the surface for nearly anything. Still, it felt good to cast one of my flies and have it taken so quickly.

I fished downstream, which is contrary to British protocol and their notions of sportsmanship, but I didn't care. The British claim one must fish upstream, preferably casting to visible fish, but a Hornberg, for my money, is always better quartered downstream and swung through the tailwater. In this instance, at least, it worked, because I caught five trout in ten casts, all of them taking solid whacks at the Hornberg as it lollygagged into the slack water. A hit on a streamer is always solid, I've found, and I cast until the pool gave up.

I continued downstream, partially because I wanted to be away from the hunters, but also because I suspected, due to my nature, that the guide at the Orvis store might have directed us upstream in order to keep the bigger, more interesting fishing to himself. That indicated a dim view of humanity on my part, but I couldn't help it. To feed my suspicion, I uncovered three pools, all healthy looking trout habitat, within a half mile of the camping spot. I kept the Hornberg on and did pretty well. One fish, the largest of the morning, hit and threw the fly after taking one spectacular leap. Through some combination of forces, it happened to reenter tail first and so made no splash at all. Had the trout been the blade of a spade, it could not have entered more sweetly.

I fished until noon, then sat on an old log and read while eating a cheese sandwich. The cheese sandwich was not very good, but the book was excellent. Birds came and studied me, then took off. After a time I put the book down and crawled onto the rocks, using my balled up fly jacket as a pillow. Years ago I heard that Picasso, after lunch, permitted himself a short nap. Apocryphal or not, the story maintained that he sat in an easy chair and held his coffee spoon just above his empty cup, which he had set on the ground at his side. When he relaxed sufficiently to loosen his grip on the spoon, it fell the few inches from his hand, clattered against the cup, woke him, and he started on his afternoon's work. I have always liked the story and stand by it even if it isn't true, primarily because I like a nap after lunch. On this day I fell asleep hard and slept about twelve minutes, the rocks like warm bones beneath me. Nellie didn't sleep, as best as I could tell. She lay next to me, her head busy scanning the countryside, her nose active in testing the wind.

Later in the day we came to a magnificent pool, one in which the central feature was a submerged log. The water ran over it in a sheer curtain, the surface water pulled as thin as fabric. I stood for a while and studied the fall of water, thinking that if I could puzzle it out correctly, the fish would volunteer readily enough. The Hornberg, happily, seemed the proper fly, because it would be sufficiently buoyant to skim over the log, then heavy enough to drop below the water when the current pushed downward. I walked downstream so I could fish back up to the log, then spent a few false casts drying the Hornberg by flicking it back and forth. When I thought it was ready, I let the fly fall on the stretched skin of water. Things happened quickly, because the water grabbed the fly and yanked it below. Then nothing occurred for a two count, and I imagined the fly drifting momentarily in relatively slack water, only to push up again toward the surface after it had hit bottom. I worried about snags, but could do little about it. When the fly moved past the bottom water, it began up again, and suddenly a fish hit. It hit hard and shot downstream, eager to be away from whatever had caused it such surprise. My line went with it. The fish porpoised three times. Eventually it swung down to the shallow water and glimmered against the rocks, a bright, native cutthroat, its gills working hard. I released it carefully.

I caught fifteen fish out of that pool. Each fish took almost exactly the same way; each took the Hornberg. The sun softened and when it struck water its reflection rode at the mercy of the current, widening and narrowing as the water changed. Near the closest bank the current sifted through a thicket of willow, and the water made a deep liquid cricket hum on the quieter air of evening.

When I finished, I dug a tennis ball out of my pocket and tossed it for Nellie. She had been patient with my fishing, but as soon as she saw the ball she became intensely interested. I lobbed it into the pool and watched her charge into the water.

She swam with the current and caught up to the ball with a chomp, then angled back and shook herself. She brought me the ball and we repeated the process three or four times. Each time she snagged the ball just before it reached the shallower, faster water. I loved to see her swim. I loved to see her retrieve, too, and have often thought that I did her an injustice by not training her as a bird dog. She loves to fetch and I have lost numerous socks and hats from her habit of carrying things to me at the oddest moments, dropping them near me even if I am not watching. Each spring I have found gloves and T-shirts soggy and waiting beneath the snow, evidence of her desire to give me things. Her mouth is always soft and the garments are never harmed except by their long sleep in the snow.

On my way back to camp, I decided to spend one last night. It was too late in the day to start for somewhere else. I hoped the elk hunters might be off hunting, but when I arrived back at camp they had a large fire going and were drinking a few beers. Nellie beat me over to them and they hooted a little when she went for some food left out, but then they called over and offered a beer.

I went. They greeted me warmly, happy to have company. The man who handed me a beer—a large man whose knuckles were as outsize as walnuts—introduced himself as Phil. The middle-sized one, a solid guy in a black cowboy hat, said he was Mike. And the last one, the smallest of the three, touched his fingers to his baseball cap and said that left him to be Rich. Rich said he had been studying the New Hampshire license plate and its motto, "Live Free Or Die," and he wondered what the hell that meant exactly. I told him I didn't know, but that we usually amended it to say Live Freeze and Die. That introduced the entire topic of weather and we were off for the next twenty minutes talking about approaching winter and the trouble you could have in the hills. I told him about our hike out over twelve thousand feet, and they answered that it wouldn't do to get caught on the mountainside of a twelve-thousand-foot pass this late in the year.

"You think you can hike out no matter what," Mike said, "but the truth is, the snow can catch you. I never go over a pass this late in the season."

"You never go into the woods this late in the season," Rich answered.

I asked about elk hunting. They said it wasn't as good as it had been, but then, what was? They offered another beer and I thanked them but said I was going to cook an early dinner and call it a night. Come back if you want a nightcap, they said. I told them I'd consider it.

I cooked up a pan of beans and rice. It was pretty good. Afterward I let Nellie clean the pan while I washed the silverware. She nosed the pan in a circle around the rear of the truck, the aluminum bumping against the rocks. I finished the dishes and then pulled on a parka and added a wool cap. We sat for awhile and did nothing at all. It had been a good day. I told Nellie we were lucky.

I told her she was a sock monster, the scourge of bedroom floors. I asked her if she remembered Gusty, her Labrador friend from her St. Paul's days, and that got her turning her head, looking for her old companion. Then I asked if she remembered Amy, the Gray Man, our former life. She edged closer and put her weight against me. We stayed that way and watched sparks come off the campfire, cinders falling into their own reflections on the water.

81

YELLOW–STONE

5:

WHEN I DROVE THROUGH the south entrance to Yellowstone National Park, it was three o'clock and already cold. Yellowstone, as anyone knows who has visited it, is a strange place. A high, anomalous plateau where sulfuric fumes mix with pine smells, it is indisputably one of the most beautiful parks in North America. The majority of visitors to Yellowstone remain on the loops of roads that meander through the park, lending it a grocery store feeling. To your left are elk, to your right, bison, and up ahead, if you're lucky, you may spot a moose. Bears occasionally waddle through the campgrounds or across roads, and when they do you have long lines of traffic complete with people jumping out of their cars to snap photographs. The campgrounds are jammed. The lines at Old Faithful, and at other well-established viewing destinations, are endless. Gift shops sell funny bumper stickers, cups and glasses shaped like wolves, plates with maps of Yellowstone painted on them. Most visitors don't seem to mind. I suspect that many of us are so accustomed to watching television that we see nothing unusual about viewing wildlife through the square windows of our vehicles. It's the Nature Channel, only better.

The first time I visited Yellowstone, five years before, I nearly died from an odd set of circumstances. I had been fishing all day, wading the Madison River and hooking a number of trout on a sink tip line and a leaded hare's ear. Most of the trout were good sized. I also hooked a fair amount of mountain whitefish, a toothless cousin of the native trout which take flies, especially nymphs, in much the same manner as trout. It had been a good day and I should have broken off in the afternoon, happy to have had my fill, but it was Yellowstone and I was simply going back to a tent, so there was no reason to end the day.

Near sunset I began picking up heavy trout along a channel undercutting a grassy bank where tourists passed by to snap photos of the wandering bison herds. More than one tourist shouted over to ask how I was doing, and I replied that it had been a good day and left it at that. After figuring out how the trout positioned themselves against the far bank, I was having uncanny luck. Standing in waist-deep water I cast a small weighted Muddler Minnow to the head of the pool, drifted it, let it bounce on the gravel two or three times, let the slack build in the loopy section of lazy water, then, just as the streamer moved past a small zone directly opposite me, bingo. The fish hit with sudden, thick heaves, as if they pulled the lines over their shoulders rather than took them in their mouths. I lost count at ten fish. In fact, the fish came so suddenly, and so regularly, that I began to fantasize that it was always the same fish, that one particularly aggressive specimen leaped off my line, then, in cartoon fashion, screamed into position again, ready for more combat.

84

An hour passed, maybe two, and when the sun had finally left I reeled in my fly line and hooked the Muddler to the rod. Deep, fluttery shudders began to migrate up from my spine and I realized, not for the first time, that I was slightly hypothermic. A day in the water, I thought, and dismissed it. But when I tried to retreat, to back away from the crescent of the pool, my legs refused to move. Specifically, my right leg felt anchored to the streambed and when I concentrated and tried to understand what had occurred, I realized that my waders—a cheap, rubber pair I had patched repeatedly—had leaked. I had been so cold that I failed to mark it, and the water had filled and swollen the rubber leg until it appeared, in the last light, as wide and as stretched as a frog's stomach. Standing still, the water in my boot was hardly noticeable. If anything, the added weight had made me more steady on my feet, so that I had cast to the trout without moving in hours.

Now, ready to depart, my foot had no sensation whatsoever, which would not have been dangerous if the force of the stream weren't pressing hard against my thighs. To escape I would have to wade twenty yards or more onto a gravel bed where I might be able to drain the water from my boot and regain a sense of balance. If I fell, a possibility that seemed more likely than not, I doubted seriously that I could right myself again. Once the bib of my waders dipped underwater, the rest of the rubber would be stuffed with liquid weight, and I would bob down to the bottom, dragged by my concentration on angling, the trout having a final ironic victory.

I saw the humor of the situation. But when I tried to shift my foot on the streambed, I couldn't lift it. I experienced what I imagine amputees experience on first waking to find their limb gone. The term for it, I remember from high school health class, is called phantom limb. The patient believes the limb is still present, despite intellectual evidence to the contrary. Similarly, I looked down through the darkening water and asked my foot to perform a task it had performed millions of times. It couldn't. I tried two or three commands, and my foot disobeyed. I remember grinning at the far bank after the third time, smiling at this inexpressible betrayal, assured that eventually circumstances would reverse themselves. It was inconceivable that my leg wouldn't work, that the weight of combined water and numbness would keep me, like Hercules, powerless if I removed my foot from the earth.

Before I could move, I heard bison galloping across the flat ground behind me. Normally I would have turned to watch, but now I was nervous about my situation. It occurred to me that I might die. Stranger accidents happened every day, and certainly anglers drowned often enough, their waders filling and dragging them down. I had never fallen in the water, not in fifteen years of fishing, and I forced myself to remember that simple fact as I clamped my fly rod in my teeth and bent close to the surface, my hands going underwater to hoist my leg.

It took me half an hour to lift, then step, lift, then step. Happily no one saw me, because I certainly must have appeared ridiculous. I faltered only once. The water had drained down to my thigh and the liquid slurp in my boot had become nearly manageable when I suddenly slipped on a smooth rock. I went down almost to one knee, my hands out like a telemark skier traversing a hillside, the fly rod quivering idiotically in my mouth. At the gravel bank I stood and let the boot disgorge its water, my shivers deep and hard. All around me the bison continued to graze, their grassy aroma like old hay in an autumn barn. It was difficult to see them. When I did spot them, it was from the absence of light their black bodies created, the outline of shadow they pulled from the pines behind them.

As I drove beside the Madison River on my way to the campground, I pointed out three elk to Nellie, but she seemed unimpressed. The bison, however, were a different matter. She liked seeing the bison, particularly when they appeared in geyser vents, their black bodies ghostly in the sulfuric mist. I tried to confuse her and tell her they were dogs, but she didn't buy it. She sat straight on the seat beside me, her nose bumping constantly against the front windshield.

The Madison campground was a flat, ugly area at the confluence of three world-class trout rivers—the Gibbon, the Firehole, and the Madison. It is sound policy to give over as little land to campgrounds as possible, but the result in this instance was a cheerless place. I kept Nellie tied securely to the picnic bench, a limitation she did not seem to mind. She sat and watched the Richardson squirrels, which were everywhere, pop in and out of the ground.

It was too late to fish, so I contented myself with setting up camp and tying a few flies. I tied a sort of Zug Bug, a black, thick-bodied insect that suggests a number of stone flies to a trout. Then, for the heck of it, I tied three dry flies using my own gray hair as the hackle. They came out looking something like an Adams, with a gray-green body and dun hackle. On the last fly I cut a swatch of Nellie's hair and used it as dubbing fur. I called the combination the Nellie Importuner and tossed it in my fly book.

The next morning I woke early and headed to Trout Lake

in the northeast quadrant of the park. Trout Lake had been where I first spotted trout in Yellowstone. Driving in from the northeast entrance on the trip I had taken five years before, the trip where my waders had filled and nearly drowned me, I had spotted a sign that said Trout Lake. I had found the name ironic, the kind of broad, unmistakable sign that one couldn't ignore if one were an angler. Needing to stretch, I had hiked without fishing gear up a thin trail the mile to the lake, prepared to simply turn around. At the top, just before reaching the water, I ran into an older gentleman who told me he had never seen so many large trout patrolling such a small body of water. He said he had seen fish pass by that went at least twenty inches, some larger. His report started a nervous gnawing in my stomach, one that I couldn't satisfy that day because I was on my way to meet someone. When I gained the lake, I squatted in the shade of a large pine and watched as one fish after another cruised the shallows, each one solid as a block of cord wood. Unfortunately, I had arranged to spend the remainder of that trip on the other side of the park and didn't have a chance to return. Trout Lake had remained an El Dorado, a mythical place in my mind that kept me awake nights. Now, with Nellie, I planned to return. I had carried my float tube two thousand miles with the express purpose of using it in Trout Lake.

The hard part was explaining to Nellie it is against park regulations to take a dog into the back country. I had asked a ranger about the policy and he had told me that dogs occasionally scout out bears and agitate them, and when the bears pursue, the dog brings the whole growling mess back to the owner. That seemed like a reasonable explanation, but I didn't much like it. Nellie wasn't pleased with it either and when I locked her in the back of the truck, she whined to come with me. I was firm with her and caved only enough to give her a biscuit. I felt selfish leaving her, but the gnawing sensation in my stomach, delayed several years, had returned. Hiking up the rooted trail to the lake, I was a happy man.

The lake sat in a bowl of hills, large pines ringing the eastern end. Druid Peak, at 9,583 feet, stood in snow to the west. My breath plumed in front of me. The temperature was in the low forties, but I still felt warm from the truck heater. I wore neoprene waders and several sweatshirts, a watch cap, sunglasses, and a pair of wool mittens. I used the aluminum case of my fly rod as a bindle stick, the float tube as a hobo's bandana. It took ten minutes to get to the lake. When I arrived I squatted in the exact position I had squatted several years before. The trout didn't disappoint me. In the first minute of my arrival, two large fish swung through the shallows, their tails moving leisurely, their size enough to make stringing my fly rod an exercise in suppressing impatience.

I tied on a weighted caddis nymph and backed into the water. For a moment, as always, I mistrusted the simplicity of the float tube. To sit in a tube, to paddle with one's feet, to have one's hands free to fish, seemed — as it did every time I took to the water in a tube — a child's cockeyed invention, the mistaken notion of a ten-year-old, leaping from the garage roof and trusting to an umbrella to float him down. But I knew from experience it worked beautifully. I kicked my way to the center of the lake, cold creeping up my knees and thighs. I did nothing at all in the middle except look around. Here, I told myself, was a good moment.

I worked up to the western end of the lake, cast three or four more times, and hooked my first trout on the retrieve. It was a heavy, solid fish, the type that lifts the line free of the water, stringing it back to the angler in one enormous tug. Immediately it began to run, knicking the leader through the roped strands of grass tethered to the lake bottom. I let it take as much line as it needed, my stomach fluttery, my hands nearly too quick. I wanted this fish. I wanted it because I knew to lose it meant that I would be haunted by it, would think about it before sleep, that any fish after this one could get away without any concern on my part, but that this first one was a test of something. That was probably overblown and silly, though that's how I felt. As the fish ran I looked at the hillsides, at the pines, and I tried to think down the line, to guess the fish's next move. When I succeeded in bringing it closer, I saw that it was big, probably somewhere around seventeen inches. It was sodden with approaching winter. I kept the rod tip up and let it fight the bend. I knew that I shouldn't permit the fish to become exhausted so that its survival was jeopardized. I pulled it closer so rapidly I risked its early escape. The hook remained solid and I held the fish submerged for a moment, a sort of handshake, then worked the hook free and let the trout slide through my fingers. It swam away crisply.

It was satisfying, and perhaps a good omen, to have the first fish of the day quickly behind me. It's rare that I catch only one fish. More common is to be shut out altogether, or to catch three or four fish in a hurry, as it happened that day. The nymph must have been the correct fly. I caught a second fish, equally as heavy as the first, in the next few minutes. A third after that. Then a fourth. For a long time I caught nothing at all. Cold began to build in my limbs and travel into my hands. A light snow started to fall. Flakes landed on the surface like white water striders. I sat for a while and watched.

When the cold became too much, I paddled back to the

shore and climbed out. Deep, wooden shivers worked through my bones. I jogged up and down the trail for a few minutes, hopping at the end of each sprint, trying to get my body heated. It worked fairly well, although every time I stopped I felt the cold tunneling through my chest. Now and then a trout rose and forced me to consider fishing from the bank.

Generally I am reluctant to start fishing again once I have stopped, especially when the earlier attempt had been successful. I decided to leave well enough alone. I packed up and hiked down to the truck. Nellie sulked when she saw me. I gave her a biscuit and let her sniff around the truck as I stripped out of my waders. I told her I had caught a few good trout. She didn't seem to care. She trotted up the hill toward the lake, tail flopping back and forth, to ask me to go for a hike. I told her she had missed this one, but I compromised and took her to a small creek that drained from the lake. Water tipped over rocks, clicking in white splashes, shelf to shelf, until the sound merged with the wind sifting through the treetops. Nellie drank. I let her roam around for awhile, her tags jingling. Somewhere I read that a dog's sense of smell is one million times more sensitive than ours. I tried to imagine what it must be like to be in a strange land, with strange plants and animals to discover, her nose drawn and pushed by scents indecipherable to us. She seemed impatient with each new smell; her snout jumped back and forth, jerking to discover a fresh scent before it had adequately tested the first. I let her run until she calmed down. She returned to the water, drinking from one pool until her tongue sounds linked to the noise of the stream. When she looked up, we both spotted the deer at the same time.

The deer stood uphill, stiff against the backdrop. Maybe it

had been there for a time, its scent driving Nellie to impatience. It was a male mulie with a large rack of antlers and a solid brown body barely lifting it free from the autumn colors behind it. It could not have been more still. Nellie let one puff of air come up from her throat, the exhalation puffing her cheeks, but she did not truly bark. She had seen deer before, naturally, but usually at a greater distance. Somehow we had ended up fairly close to this deer, the distance between us not more than a fallen birch tree.

For a moment nothing happened. Then the deer seemed to gain life in its ankles and it trotted away, moving swiftly, its head ducking slightly to move beneath the trees. Nellie took two steps and I told her no, leave it, and she did. I watched the deer, thinking that I would be able to note the exact moment it disappeared, but a combination of the gloomy day and the brown background made the deer seem to vanish. I looked at Nellie to determine if she still saw it. I couldn't say if she did or not.

She bent back to the water. I slapped my thigh and we walked back to the truck. While I had been fishing, the temperature had dropped. Although it was only mid-afternoon, cold had soaked down through the higher elevations and had covered the valleys. At first I thought I was merely chilled from fishing, but when I checked my thermometer it registered in the thirties. Given the temperature and the long afternoon and evening in front of me, I decided to have dinner at the Old Faithful Lodge, one of my favorite places in the world. Old Faithful Lodge is, of course, a tourist center, but that doesn't diminish the beauty of its construction. Built of interlocking pine beams around magnificent stone hearths, the upper floors stretching skyward nearly beyond view, it is one of the true grand hotels in our nation. It took me an hour to meander through the park, stopping frequently for construction along the Madison–West Thumb stretch of road, before I entered the Old Faithful visitor center. By the time I arrived, despite the warmth from the truck's heater, the cold had soaked into my bones.

I left Nellie in the truck and went in to take a shower. It's a little known secret that one can pay a minimal fee and take a shower in the Old Faithful Lodge. Perhaps it started as a service for hikers and campers, but in any case the desk manager did not flinch when I requested a towel and soap. I paid the fee, then followed his instructions to a private bath down the long hall on the first floor.

It had been a while since I had showered. I tried to calculate backward, but came up with nothing definitive. I lingered in the shower long past any decent period, then dressed in fresh clothes and went out and sat beside the large central fireplace. I considered getting a newspaper—I had been fairly out of touch for the past couple weeks—but then, without any active decision, found myself content to simply sit and stare at the flames. The wood smoke smelled western and sharp and fragrant.

I felt happy; I felt revived. The Aborigines in Australia believe in the restorative power of walkabout, the periodic benefit of abandoning one's routines and admitting the need of an individual to exist on a more physical basis for a time so that the mind might be cleansed. Obviously it is a much more complex notion to the Aborigines, and I was in a Dodge Dakota, not in the outback, but for a moment I may have understood a little of what was at the center of that power. It counts for something to get away from our usual routine. It counts to get outdoors. Most of my life I had felt an urge to light out, to get away, to travel simply to be in motion, and I had given in to it repeatedly. Sitting beside the fire, I no longer felt guilty about that. Trout streams provided an excuse to go, and luckily the streams existed, by and large, in beautiful country, but I might have just as easily traveled to collect rare walking sticks, or antique sideboards, or copies of first edition books. It didn't matter. I had been going before I discovered fishing and would continue to go if my legs could no longer connect me with water. I traveled for the contentment I experienced sitting next to the fire in the Old Faithful Lodge, for the acknowledgment that travel forced on me that I was alive, that I lived in a period of history, that I would soon be, as James Joyce said, a shade.

I roused myself and went into the bar where I ordered a bowl of pasta and a glass of scotch. I watched a little football on the TV. I ate some nuts. When the food arrived, I devoured it with what used to be called a cunning appetite. Now and then, in the quiet moments, I felt the trout-taking in Trout Lake. I pictured the line going up, connecting me with a fish, felt the frantic, waggy run of them as they scattered from my fly.

That night, in the back of the truck, I discovered two lumps on Nellie. I felt them for a moment without realizing what they were. Rubbing her belly while reading, my hand had traveled up to her ribs and at first I took the bumps to be nothing more than the xylophone of bone beneath her skin. But then my fingers probed a bit more and I put aside my book. "Good girl," I said to keep her steady, then sat up and shined my flashlight on her side. I couldn't make out much, but yes, she had more lumps. I smoothed her fur and continued petting her, this time with more purpose. I found one more spot on her shoulder.

None of the spots seemed tender. She continued snoring through most of the examination, her front paw occasionally lifting to push my hand to continue.

The next morning I made her stand on the tailgate for a beauty shop, our phrase for a brush out. Wicking her fur, I found the lumps immediately. They were not large. Twice while I inspected the lumps she licked my hand. I finished the beauty shop, then gave her breakfast while I considered my options. There was little I could do, I concluded. I remembered a Scottish expression I had always liked. It said that each person had to *dree his weird*, which meant that we all must live our fate. Nellie was no different. Besides, her appetite was good and her spirits strong. I decided to keep an eye on the lumps, but otherwise to put them out of mind as much as possible.

We spent the morning fishing the Yellowstone, which in some sense is the Mecca of fly-fishing in America. The river churns through the heart of the park, falling from Yellowstone Lake and the Fishing Bridge into the Grand Canyon of the Yellowstone. The stretch from Le Hardy Rapids to the Pelican Valley provides the potential for superb fishing. Anyone with waders and a pair of polarized sunglasses can walk halfway into the river and look down to see spectacular trout. The trout run from fourteen to twenty inches, all of them facing south, one after another, beads of fish in a net of water. The Yellowstone is closed until well after the spawning is finished in August, which makes for a relatively small window of opportunity. Anglers from around the world come to the Yellowstone in August, September, and October. On the day that I fished it, I stood shoulder to shoulder with a group of five men from Germany.

On the two trips I've made out West, I've never had much

luck on the Yellowstone. Frankly, I've rarely seen anyone catch many fish, although anglers talk about the magic of the Yellowstone. My sense is that the fish are big and the bait is small. The few fish I've caught have all been taken on midges. Only once did I ever cast a dry fly and have the fish rise to it. Otherwise the fishing has been on the bottom, a matter of drifting minuscule caddis nymphs and stone flies to remarkably uncooperative trout. It is one thing to have a poor day when you are fishing on an eastern pond, the fish below your hook six to twelve inches. It is another thing altogether to fish over enormous trout, trout that are stacked up throughout the river, trout that are perhaps the best trout in the lower forty-eight states, and catch nothing.

I brought Nellie with me down to the river and put her in a down-stay beside a large log on the shore. It was late morning. The thermometer read forty-one degrees. I sat on the log and tied a pink shrimp onto a light tippet. A dozen anglers already worked the water, none having any luck that I could see. Out of curiosity, I did some quick estimates about the money involved on the river that morning. Not counting the cost of travel to get to Yellowstone, which in the case of the Germans would be considerable, a conservative estimate put the average cost for each angler to step to the water at somewhere around $500. That was on the cheap side. The anglers wore neoprene waders, fly vests, flies, boots, and carried fly rods. A single fly rod could cost more than $500, I knew, so it was possible the total cost could be double. In any case, I calculated that at least $6,000 was represented on the water that morning. It was strange to think in those terms. Certainly fly-fishing was not as expensive as yachting, or even Alpine skiing, but the cost was not negligible. My own kit, when I ran it through a calculator, came out at about $600. The one expensive rod I had owned—an Orvis Henry's Fork—had broken in an accident years before, shortly before Orvis instituted its policy of unconditional guarantee. Now I used utilitarian rods and the cheapest flies I could find. Each year, in fact, left me feeling less and less interested in the nuances of equipment and more and more annoyed with people who turn fishing into a shopping trip. Nevertheless, if I added up the cost for trips I had taken, equipment lost, time spent away from work, it probably came to $20,000. Measured against the pleasure I had gained over twenty years of fishing, it hardly seemed exorbitant.

On my first cast I had a strike, then didn't have another nibble throughout the morning. Nellie had more luck. Whenever a new angler arrived, or a wet one left the water, he made his way to the log and sat with her. She hammed it up, of course. Two girls came down with their dad and asked if they could take her for a walk. I said it was fine as long as it was in the immediate area where I could watch. Their dad said the girls had a dog at home so it should be okay. Nellie yanked them through a pine grove for a few minutes, then towed them back to the log.

Near noon I took a break and sat with Nellie eating a sandwich when a bunch of car doors slammed on the road above the river. It was a fairly busy place, but I wasn't prepared for a group of ten to file down the dirt path. Nellie got to her feet and waited to be greeted, but this time the men passed her by and went directly into the water. It took a moment to understand what was going on, until a chubby fellow in an enormous pair of waders began shouting down the line that we had a nice tri-co hatch on. Another fellow at the other end asked the first fellow if he thought so, was he sure? Listening to them I realized that I was witnessing a group lesson, something I had never seen before. The men in line between the two guides were mostly beginners. Their casts were wobbly. Now and then they got hooked on their clothing, or threw a bee swarm of line around their heads. When they did, the guides splashed over to them and sorted things out. Throughout the session the guides shouted back and forth about the hatch, what might be expected, how the trout might be taking. Tri-cos seemed to be the order of the day, though no one caught anything while I watched.

Maybe it was because I was having no luck in any case, but I decided I had had enough of the Yellowstone. The sight of a group lesson ruined the day. I didn't like how quickly they had entered the water. I didn't like the two guides shouting up and down the river, the beginners holding out their rods to the guides to have them untangled, the lecture about feeding habits as the men fished. The guides were teaching them everything, I thought, and nothing at all. Like an old grump, I led Nellie back to the truck. I gave her a few biscuits and told her she was a good girl. My plan had been to fish the Madison and the Firehole, going to the other Yellowstone spots I remembered, but I decided instead that I was finished with Yellowstone. I was finished with the traffic, with the crowded campgrounds, with group lessons on the exquisite streams. I knew a place I wanted to try. The next fish, as always, was better than the last.

6: IDAHO

IT MUST HAVE BEEN FATE that I came across the story of Greyfriar's Bobby while preparing for this trip with Nellie. As a boy I had read Albert Payson Terhune's Lad stories, and of course Wilson Rawls's wonderful *Where the Red Fern Grows*, but it had been years since I read stories about dogs. The legend of Greyfriar's Bobby, when I spotted it in a used bookstore, seemed too improbable to be true. The story was printed on a single page in a general reference book called *The AKC's World of the Pure Bred Dog.* I had no intention of buying the book and was only thumbing through it for pictures of Golden Retrievers. Then a small sidebar on page 194 caught my attention. The sidebar explained that a statue had been erected in Edinburgh, Scotland, to commemorate a dog's devotion to man. Every day for fourteen years, from 1858 to 1872, Bobby stood vigil over his master's grave in Greyfriar's Churchyard. The statue, from what I could make out in the poor photograph, seemed to be a simple column with the figure of a small seated dog on top. Its fur was rough. It appeared to be a terrier, although I couldn't be certain.

The story struck me and I wondered how I had never heard of it before. I especially wondered if it could possibly be true. On a whim I called the American Kennel Club library and asked about it. The librarian there had never heard of Greyfriar's Bobby either, but she happily checked the library's database and came up with three book titles. An early account, published in 1929 and reprinted in 1940, was written by Eleanor Stackhouse Atkinson. Entitled simply *Greyfriar's Bobby*, it looked to be, according to the librarian, a children's story. *The True Story of Greyfriar's Bobby*, by Henry T. Hutton, came out in 1902 and was only twenty-nine pages long. With its serious, scholarly tone, it seemed intent on putting the matter of Greyfriar's Bobby straight. And finally Ruth Brown, a water-colorist, published *The Ghost of Greyfriar's Bobby* in 1995.

I asked the librarian if she had any of the books on hand and she said no. I called the University of New Hampshire library and the interlibrary loan librarian said the two earlier books were available. The Atkinson book was in the special holdings section of the state library; the twenty-nine-page account by Hutton was at the Washington State University library. I asked to borrow both, then I called my local bookstore and ordered the Ruth Brown book.

I saved these books as a treat, because I knew being on the road with Nellie would put me in the mood for dog books. But I had forgotten about them until I arrived in Ashton, Idaho. A friend had recommended Idaho in general and the Henry's Fork River specifically. I discovered an excellent campground on the Falls River at the edge of Targee National Forest, a short drive away from the Henry's Fork. My designated spot, pointed out by two retired park hosts, sat on a grassy lawn that formed a perfect terrace above the ambling current. After the crowding at

Yellowstone, I was happy to see that only one tent site was occupied, and that by a sagging lean-to that appeared to be abandoned. Pulling into my spot, I felt luxurious and comfortable. I backed around and fussed in order to get the rear of the truck to overlook the water. Then, taking my time, I erected my tent, threw my baggage in it, then carefully laid out my cooking things. Nellie sat and watched, occasionally ducking off to wade in the river and drink. It was during my unpacking that I came across the Greyfriar's Bobby books tucked away beneath a bunch of maps. A fishing trip could be flavored by what one read. My sense was that this was the place to read about dogs.

At dinnertime the campground host, Dale, came to my site and said that he saw I was a fisherman. He was a tall, slender man, the kind who stays thin by working on engines. Retired three years from California where he was a fleet mechanic for a large shipping company, he and his wife, Jess, now spent summers in Idaho living as campground hosts. He liked this particular spot, he said, and he wanted me to know that the fishing was pretty good directly behind the campground.

"I don't fish, myself," he said, "and neither does my wife. Most people go over to the Henry's Fork, but I figured you might like to know."

I told him I had been traveling for about three weeks and the prospect of sitting still for awhile was appealing.

"This is the place to do it," he said, "although we'll be closing the campground the first week of October."

"Any bears?" I asked.

"Some," he said. "They'll be denning soon, though."

After dinner I strung up my fly rod. I didn't bother with waders, thinking that if there were fish in any number, which I doubted, I could come back tomorrow to take them on seriously.

I walked Nellie up a railroad bed that followed the Falls River, watching her movement. She appeared completely recovered from our hike into the Wind River Range. She weaved back and forth, checking both sides of the railroad bed, her tail a white spot among the grasses. Each time she crossed tracks she checked to make sure I was with her, her glance precise but hasty. We had hiked a thousand miles like this, but I still took pleasure in seeing her move ahead of me. I knew if we came to a fork in the road she would sit and wait, never being stupid, always being wise about such things. More than once I had told her to take us home and then stood back to let her lead us. Now, as we walked, I let her zigzag across the trail, her steady eagerness joyful to watch.

The rail bed led to a smooth portion of the river just above a small dam, no more than two hundred yards from my campsite. In the late light the water flowed the color of tea, but I suspected that during midday hours the water would glimmer over the red, rocky bottom. I veered off to the right and climbed down a muddy bank, then stopped on a wide, pebbled beach. The river bent in a pizza crust to my right, the farthest edge the thickest and deepest. Trout rose everywhere I looked.

A thousand trout. A million trout. I could not believe my good fortune. As I stood quietly and listened, I heard the gurgle of water passing over rocks, the sound snapped to life by the quick surge of trout. I guessed the fish were small, but it would be difficult to imagine a more perfect half mile of trout water. Again I thought of the trout cocking their lateral fins into the current, the flow of water rocketing them up. The rings of their feeding drifted above them, then disappeared in the water's pull. I remembered André Gide's line: "Fish die belly-up and rise to the surface; it is their way of falling."

I forced myself to watch the water for five minutes before I cast so that I would not put them down in my hurry to fish. One particularly aggressive trout broke the easy roll of water against the far bank. It rose repeatedly, whacking at something that drifted in an eddy beneath a fallen branch. Terrestrial, I thought, but wasn't sure. I turned over a few rocks and examined the bug life beneath. A small black gnat flicked around my ankles. On an eastern stream I might have tried a weighted caddis nymph, but the moment was too good to fish with a submerged fly. I tied on a size twenty hair-wing fly, a tiny black dot, then waded in to my ankles. Nellie came out of the grasses and stood beside me, her fur drizzling, her tongue occasionally dipping to take a drink.

I didn't catch a thing. Not at first. I cast a dozen times to the rising fish near the fallen branch, but it fed next to the fly and ignored my cast altogether. I started to smile. The sun had left the sky and I stood on the bank in the cool evening light, my breath visible, cold creeping into my movement. I cursed that I hadn't worn my waders. I cursed that I hadn't dressed more warmly, but I hadn't anticipated this many trout. After a while, I abandoned the aggressive fish against the far bank and drifted a fly through a small ripple above me. A trout hit. It hit with a short, nervous take, then spit the fly back to the surface. It had been a small fish. I cast three times for it, then returned to the fish against the far bank. On the tenth or twentieth cast, I decided to change flies. Holding the tippet at eye level, the light nearly gone, I snipped off the hair-wing fly and tied on a gray-black midge.

I knew before the fly landed near the rising fish that it would take it. I'm not sure how I knew, but I did. The fly had barely settled on the water when the trout had it, its run through the main body of the river explosive. It felt surprisingly heavy, not at all like the miniature tug of a fingerling. The leader sawed the water surface.

I don't want to make too much of what happened next, but it had a strong impact on me. When I played the fish within reach, I stooped to unhook it. Naturally I examined the fish quickly, expecting to find a cutthroat or rainbow, perhaps even a brookie. What I found instead was a golden trout. At least it appeared to be a golden trout. I had heard about golden trout before and knew of their existence, but I had never seen one. I had certainly never caught one. For a moment I lifted it free of the water. The fish did indeed appear golden. It had the general shape of a ten-inch rainbow, slender and thin where a cutthroat may be slightly blunt, but gold radiated from its sides. I would have given a great deal to have had someone beside me, some-one who could have confirmed or dismissed my observation. I held the trout free of the water. Nellie sniffed it. I had always associated golden trout with California and although I had now crossed the Continental Divide, I considered it improbable that I had caught a golden trout. I knew that the Bighorn Mountains held some golden trout, but I was a long way from them.

I released it and stood. Fish still rose everywhere, but I was finished with them for the evening. I wondered if the entire section of the river was populated by golden trout. It was possible that golden trout were more common than I imagined. I remembered in Nova Scotia hearing about a lobsterman who pulled up a blue lobster, something the local papers said was a one in ten million possibility. I doubted a golden trout was as rare, but it was still rare to me.

I told Nellie we were done for the night. She seemed grateful. We took our time going back down the railroad bed, adjusting to the easy gait we always assumed on our last walk of the night. Bats wicked the air above us. I felt cold and ready for bed. Each time Nellie returned to me she smelled more strongly of the sage and mint that must have grown near the water's edge. After awhile she stopped crossing the tracks and wandered with me at a companionable speed. The mountains rose black above us and the moon came up behind the trees. I told Nellie this was one of the good nights. I let my hand dangle to tickle her head when it came close.

Back at the truck, I made a cup of tea and pulled my camp chair next to the water. It was a pretty night, although cold. I put off reading about Greyfriar's Bobby and gobbled down a few pages of Marquand instead. Reading him made me want a martini. I found a bottle of scotch and poured out a few fingers worth. I read and drank and fiddled with Nellie. For the first time since I had left, I thought seriously about going home. I thought about being in my house, beside a fire, a comfortable bed waiting. And I thought of breakfast the next morning at the Trolley Car, the local restaurant in my New Hampshire town, how the eggs would be scrambled, the home fries cut with onions and peppers. I thought about going to the grocery store and picking up the paper, maybe sitting in the park in the sun and reading it. And I thought with longing of the wooden floor in the local hardware store, how it would crackle a little with the new cold air, how the seed and garden supplies would have surrendered to andirons and starter logs.

I had heard a radio program the day before about home sickness at summer camps. One of the camp directors said that term, *home sickness*, connoted something dysfunctional, and that the better term, used now in the camping industry, was *home missing*. So I settled for that definition. Sitting beside the water, I was home missing. The cold, though, didn't let me dwell for long on the subject. I took Nellie on last rounds, then told her I was going to read her a story about dogs. When she heard the word dog, she looked around for Gusty, her old playmate.

Later, I climbed into the back of the truck, set Nellie up on her cedar bed, then pushed deep into my sleeping bag. The thermometer on my jacket said it had broken into the low thirties. The next morning, when I woke, my water bottle had a neck of ice.

It was an old feeling to read a dog book by flashlight. *The True Story of Greyfriar's Bobby* by Henry T. Hutton was not a book at all but something closer to an abstract. The leaves smelled old and musty, and when I wet my finger to turn a page, I tasted libraries. I remembered the taste from the old Hardy Boy books I had read as a kid; remembered, actually the books I had read on the screen porch all those years before the summer my mother had taken me to Mindowaskin Pond. I've included Bobby's text here. The language is old-fashioned, the punctuation inconsistent, but that adds to the account's charm. The possessive *'s* in Greyfriar's seems to jump back and forth. I've transcribed the abstract exactly as I received it.

The Memorial Fountain bears the
following inscription

GREYFRIAR'S BOBBY

FROM THE LIFE,
JUST BEFORE HIS DEATH

A TRIBUTE

TO THE AFFECTIONATE FIDELITY OF

GREYFRIAR'S BOBBY

---

*In 1858 this faithful dog followed the remains
of his master to Greyfriar's Churchyard, and
lingered near the spot until his death in 1872*

WITH PERMISSION
ERECTED BY THE
BARONESS BURDETT-COUTTS
1872

In the pages of "Dog Stories" from the *Spectator*
published in 1896, there appeared a brief and passing
reference to the subject of this sketch, a faithful Skye
terrier, known from the romance of his life as "Greyfriars'
Bobby." The characteristic fidelity which marked the
career of this notable dog has found recognition in the

form of a memorial fountain placed near George IV.
Bridge, one of the leading thoroughfares of old Edinburgh, close to the gate of Greyfriar's Church.

GREYFRIARS' BOBBY

During the "fifties" there lived in Midlothian a farmer
named Gray. This man, like others of his calling, was
generally to be found in Edinburgh every Wednesday,
attending the market, accompanied always by his shaggy
terrier "Bobby." It was Gray's custom, as the time-gun
announced the hour of one from the Castle heights,
to repair to a small restaurant in the neighborhood of
Greyfriars' Churchyard, known by the name of Traill's
Dining-rooms. Here Bobby and his master had their
midday meal, which in the case of the doggie consisted
regularly of a bun, probably followed by a canine *bonne
bouche* in the way of a bone.

In 1858 Gray died, and was laid to rest in the historic
churchyard of Grayfriars, aptly named by Sir Walter Scot
"the Westminster of Scotland." On the third day following the funeral, and just as the echoes of the time-gun
were dying away, the occupants of Traill's rooms were
surprised to see a dog, the picture of woe and hunger,
enter the doorway and approach the proprietor, upon
whom he gazed with a most beseeching expression.

Traill immediately recognised in this visitor the
once happy and well-cared-for Bobby. Stirred with com-
passion, he gave a bun to the silent pleader, who then,
without waiting to eat it, ran out of the shop, carrying his
newly-found meal in his mouth. Next day, at the same
hour, Bobby again appeared, and a repetition of events
followed; but on the third day, Traill, whose curiosity

and interest were now thoroughly aroused, determined to follow the dog, and thus discover his destination. This was soon reached, for Bobby, bun in mouth, made straight for Greyfriars' Churchyard, where, approaching the grave of his master, he lay down and began to eat his scanty meal. It was now evident that a chief, if not only mourner of the kind-hearted farmer, had been his four-footed friend Bobby, who, after following his late master's funeral, had then refused to leave the newly formed mound which marked his grave, until forced to do so by the pangs of hunger. Bobby's plight, and the locality of his new domicile, having come to the knowledge of the occupants of his former home, he was brought back, it is said, three times. However, all efforts to make him relinquish his chosen post proved unavailing, and each attempt was followed by a speedy return to the same spot in Greyfriars.

It is on record that James Brown, the old groundkeeper and superintendent at Greyfriars viewed, with mingled kindness and perplexity, what, in face of the gateway notice "Dogs not admitted," constituted an unallowable intrusion. Hitherto old James had put forth his best efforts to enforce this rule; Bobby, however, was now made the exception, and, from having been an unconscious violator of sanctuary, such then did Greyfriars become to him and remained so till the end of his life. Here, at or near his master's grave, Bobby continued to spend both days and nights, taking refuge only in rough weather under a tombstone hard by, and stoutly resisting all friendly advances made by compassionate strangers desirous of providing a home for him. Confirmation as to Bobby's night-time habitat is shown in the letter of a Heriot "Old Boy" written years ago, in which—alluding to various nocturnal escapades of his school-days—he wrote "... we used to climb over the wall of Greyfriars' Churchyard and skip across, but you didn't go very far before Bobby was at your heels and a proper yelping he set up and he never stopped till we were over the Hospital wall." In course of time a shelter was erected for Bobby's protection near his master's grave. He continued his daily visits to the restaurant, arriving punctually at the same hour, and never failing to receive his bun from the kind-hearted proprietor. This went on for nine years, when, owing to a more rigorous enforcement of the seven shillings yearly dog licence, Bobby was arrested as a "vagrant," and appeared in Court, accompanied by his humane sympathiser and defender, the restaurant keeper, who was accused of "harboring" the dog. They were tried before three magistrates, who, after hearing the story, tempered the law with mercy, and forgave him for not paying his rates, thus saving Bobby from an untimely end.

The then Lord Provost, William Chambers, happening to enter the Court and having heard the story, said he would be responsible for the payment of the licence and, moreover, further practically extended his interest by having a collar made for Bobby with the inscription on a brass plate as follows: "Greyfriars' Bobby from The Lord Provost, 1867, Licensed." The actual collar, as here illustrated, was, after Bobby's death, deposited in the City Museum, where it can now be seen. This kind-hearted Lord Provost—who, with his brother Robert Chambers, remains eminent in the annals both of literature and those of Edinburgh—continued, true to his word, to effect the annual renewal of the licence the remaining years of Bobby's life.

110

It may be of interest to mention here that a baronetcy was offered to and accepted by Lord Provost Chambers; but he died before the distinction was conferred.

But to return to Bobby. This remarkable dog who, by an irony of fate, had great length of days granted to him, lived until 1872, and then, like his master, was buried in Greyfriars's Churchyard, where his not far distant grave, in a flower bed near the main entrance, is often pointed out to visitors.

It is worthy of note that, within a very few yards from this spot, perpetuating as it does the devotion of a so called "lower being" to his earthly master, is located the memorable group of graves here illustrated and where, it is reputed, upon whose now time-worn slabs, did those stalwarts of Scottish religious history — the precursors of hundreds who, many years later, were kept for months rigorously and harshly imprisoned in a roofless enclosure near-by in the graveyard — sign, on the 1st of March 1638, many of them with blood drawn from their own veins, the great National Covenant, thus testifying to *their* unbreakable faith in Him, the Almighty Master of all.

A short time before Bobby's death the Baroness Burdett-Coutts visited Greyfriars, and the sight of the Highland mourner so interested her, that when his demise occurred, she obtained permission to erect at the street corner, near the Churchyard gate, a granite fountain with an effigy of the inconsolable dog sitting on guard, as depicted in the frontispiece.

In addition to being thus memorialised in bronze, Bobby also had the distinction of being the subject for the brush of various artists, one of them being the late

Mr. John McLeod who, in 1868, exhibited at the Royal
Scottish Academy a pictured entitled "Greyfriars' Bob
(No. 705 — the property of Thos. Cowan, Esq.) A
pleasing sketch in oils, of Bobby, by the same artist, will
be found inside the Session House within Old
Greyfriars' Church. Another portrayer of Bobby was the
late Mr. Gourlay Steell.

Bobby had many friends, amongst them being
Sergeant Scott of the Royal Engineers, by whom a
weekly treat of steaks was long allowed to him in
addition to his daily kind bounty from Mr. Traill.

Thus did a kind Humanity — in recognition of mute
but eloquent faithfulness — accord to Bobby tribute
quite unique.

I have come now to the end of my simple narrative.
Perhaps it may remind the reader, as it did the writer, of
the affectionate dog and his master, who, in the words of
the poet: —

> *But thinks, admitted to that equal sky,*
> *His faithful dog shall bear him company.*

Finishing Hutton's abstract, I turned off my flashlight and
thought of Porky, a beagle mix, the dog of my childhood. My
brother John brought her home, claiming, as family legend still
has it, that he had found her along the road and could not outrun her. He could not outrun her litter mate, either, a brown and
white beagle named Bess. It was years later, when I learned a
little about music, that I realized we had named the dogs after
the folk opera, *Porgy & Bess*. It had been a popular show at the

time, but as a child I had unknowingly converted the name to Porky. Bess died in a tragic accident. My second oldest brother, Chuck, went up for a rebound in a backyard basketball game and came down on Bess when she was just a puppy. He broke the dog's back or neck. Bess *went to sleep*, I was told.

Porky survived in a family of seven children. Porky was black and white with two brown spots above her eyes, and a wide plump body that was woefully out of shape. I thought of Porky after reading about Greyfriar's Bobby because Porky, as my childhood dog, was the dog of my wishes.

One Saturday morning my father had been raking and when he turned a turtle over he called me to examine it. I must have been five or six. The yellow spots on the turtle, the wide carapace, the decided weight of the turtle as it dangled in the grappling hooks of my childish fingers, fascinated me. Immediately I wanted it for a pet. I asked my dad what a turtle likely ate, and he told me lettuce, maybe celery. I knew we had a cardboard box in the garage; I knew where to get food. I put the turtle down, asked my dad to watch it, then ran inside. It probably took me some time, but when I returned I expected the turtle to be where I had left it. It was gone, of course. I yelled at my father, suspecting that he had moved it. He told me no, he had simply returned to raking. He helped me look but eventually shrugged that it was gone. He did not admonish me for yelling at him, as he normally would have, and I have always taken that as proof of his guilt.

Determined to find the turtle, I turned to Porky. Whether I had the notion from TV—"Rin Tin Tin" was a popular show around that time—or from books, I believed Porky could find the turtle. I called her to me and got on my knees in front of her. Turtle, I said over and over to her. Find the turtle. I'm certain I was crying. She patiently sat, thus performing her one trick and expected to receive a biscuit. No, no, no, I said. Find the turtle. I dragged her to the spot where the turtle had been and made her smell the area, figuring, in my TV–addled mind, that she would understand what I needed. Passionately I implored her to find it. Please, Porky, please please please.

She didn't understand a thing, naturally. She wandered in circles, sniffed a little, then kept sitting in front of me, begging for biscuits. I sank my face in her fur, whispered to her, pleaded with her to do this one thing. My heart hurt. I eventually sobbed into her fur, clinging to her neck, repeating over and over my request. Why did I want the turtle so much? I have no idea. But I wanted, equally, the understanding from Porky, the communication, the hope she brought. All the dog stories in the world are about Porky finding the turtle.

The great luxury of fishing in the West is that one can start much later in the morning, at ten or eleven, and still have a successful day. The morning after reading the accounts of Greyfriar's Bobby, a Saturday, I woke feeling lazy and peaceful. I was also hungry. I made a quick trip into the Ashton Bestway, purchased the local newspaper, eggs, and bacon, then spent an hour or two poking around my Coleman stove, cooking. Nellie watched me cook with an attentive eye, ready to scrounge around my feet if I dropped any crumbs. When I finished, I gave her an egg sandwich. She ate it in three or four good bites, then curled up and went to sleep, her tail in the sun, her nose neatly capped by a leaf.

On my second cup of coffee, Dale stopped by. He refused

my offer of coffee. He was on his way to cut some grass. I told him about the golden trout—feeling slightly foolish as I did so—but he simply shrugged and said he guessed it was possible. Then I asked where the best place might be to watch a football game on television, Tennessee vs. Florida State, and he recommended one of the two bars in downtown Ashton. As he left, I felt like a rich man. After a wonderful, leisurely breakfast, I could fish for a few hours, then totter to town and drink a few beers while watching what promised to be an excellent football game. Moreover, I felt I could use the company. Since Bob and Tom's departure in Dubois, I had been traveling alone. Although I agreed with Thoreau, who said, "I never found the companion that was so companionable as solitude," the notion of a bar and a few peanuts held a strong appeal. It also occurred to me that I might find out a little about the Henry's Fork and come up with other places to fish the following day.

By eleven I was on the water, this time properly outfitted in waders and warm clothes. After she explored the river a half mile in either direction, Nellie stood beside me, chin pressed against my knee. Shade covered the water. Fish rose as adamantly as they had the previous night. Because of my calm morning, I fished patiently and with extremely small terminal tackle. I cast upstream, letting a gold caddis nymph tick along the bottom. Almost immediately I began picking up fish. They were all about eight inches. Each fought with frantic energy, tailing across pools, running at me as often as running away. Nellie examined each fish when I brought it to hand. Not one was golden.

After a while I began to feel I was an expert fisherman. It's a well-known liability among anglers, an affliction to which I am particularly susceptible. One night on the Deerfield River in Massachusetts I happened to be present when a wonderful hatch of March browns occurred. The flies were big, grumpy looking things that replicated three or four ugly Wulfs I had tied myself and had with me in my fly book. The trout, to my delight, rose about forty or fifty feet away. Most fishing occurs within a short cast from an angler's feet. But on the Deerfield that night I was able to crank it up, to cast a large fly to the limit of my fly rod, then let the fly flutter onto the surface to be met by a cooperative fourteen-inch rainbow. In the time it took to hook three fish, I became a pro. Instantly, all the evenings I had struggled, all the days I had been skunked, became the anomalies. That night, I concluded, was the true measure of my fishing. But the next evening I returned to the same spot, often a mistake, and, after enormous effort, caught a few lousy trout in the tailwaters, long after my fly had sunk in the swirls at the end of the run. As quickly as that, I was mortal again.

The same inflation I experienced on the Deerfield began to occur on the Falls River, a mile above my campground. I was the trout master. How easy to read water! How simple to seduce trout! After the fourth or fifth fish, I decided catching them with a small nymph was not good enough. I sat on the bank and tied on an Adams, a brown-gray fly nearly twice the size of the nymph. Nellie sat beside me, her fur wet and smelly. She was not impressed with my success and she kept her eyes moving over the far side of the river, watching the day move across the hillside. When I waded back into the stream I fished not with anticipation, but with the satisfaction of a man waiting on a good payday. The work of studying the river and figuring out the essentials was already accomplished. I cast the Adams, lifting the rod tip at the end of each probe just a little so that the fly landed first. I crouched a bit so my silhouette would not spook the trout. I fished beautifully, I thought, but absolutely without result.

It didn't matter. A minor setback. I changed to a small mosquito and repeated the process. I even allowed the fly to dip under the water surface—a tactic that is not considered good form because it supposedly makes the fly nearly irresistible to the fish—and felt my mortality returning to me at a gallop. Naturally I fished less well now that my confidence had diminished. The trout that had been so cooperative fifteen minutes before suddenly seemed otherwise engaged. After striking out with the mosquito, I humbly returned to the small golden caddis I had been successful with earlier in the morning. I cast it out and let it drift the same way as before. This time, if anything, I demonstrated more care in its presentation. The trout ignored it. Not only did they ignore it, but they began rising around it, as if escorting it to the end of the run. I couldn't help feeling they weren't taking me seriously. There was no good reason they would refuse the same fly they had eagerly taken thirty minutes before. I promised myself I would catch one more, then I would knock off to watch the football game.

It took close to two hours to get the last fish. I changed flies four more times, went back to the original caddis nymph, used the fly I had succeeded with the night before, came back to the caddis nymph, tried bright, gaudy, ridiculous flies, streamers, ants, then finally hooked a ten-inch cutthroat on a wooly bugger beneath a log that lay half-submerged in the water. I played that fish as carefully as I had ever played a fish, because I knew, intuitively, that my perverse nature in these matters would force me to catch another fish before I left the stream unless I brought this one to hand. I played the fish like a man carrying hot soup. When I finally released it, I reeled in and tied off the line. The trout had not ceased rising.

Nellie led me back to camp. I took a few minutes to wash, splashing in the stream until I felt at least marginally better. Whenever my attention wavered from the immediate task at hand, images of rising trout spooked me. I had to shake them out of my head. Vainglorious, I told myself. That's what I had been. That was why they continued to taunt me.

I stored everything in the tent, then climbed into the truck and headed into town. Nellie sat beside me, happy to go for a ride. Her ears rode the wind passing through the truck.

I'm not sure how the conversation about leg wrestling began, but I think it was a standing joke that I fell into without knowing what I was doing. Ashton, Idaho, is a small town, a very small town. It consists of a few businesses along Route 20—the Bestway, a couple convenience stores—and a main street. The main street forms a T against Route 20, with a stop sign that effectually eliminates the chance that someone would accidentally drive through the town without stopping. A large potato-processing plant takes up one side of the downtown area. I am not sure what I had been expecting—maybe a bright, oak wood bar with a lively crowd, some funny drinks named after regular customers, a nacho special for the football game—but the prospects for watching the game dulled considerably when I found the two bars to which Dale had directed me. The sports type bar that Dale felt was my best bet was closed. It didn't appear to have been opened in the last twenty years. The door was boarded. Someone had soaped the windows.

The other bar, located across the street, was the kind of place that was dark at noon and bright at midnight. It was the kind of place where you put cigarettes out on the floor, then walked across the butts later, feeling as though you were crushing thick beetles. It had five draft pulls, all serving Bud or Miller. It had a sign that said no drinking until after five, and all the numbers on the clock were five.

I walked in and sat at the end of the bar, directly beneath the television. I was not the only customer. Two silent men sat at the other end of the bar, both of them wearing cowboy hats, both of them with Skoal cans bulging in their rear pockets.

Sharon ran the place. A short, dark-haired woman in her early forties, she sat beneath the TV smoking and reading magazines. She had a swarm of magazines. She told me customers brought in magazines from home and left them at the bar for her. Skimming pages, cutting things out, she fanned through *Readers Digest, Glamour, Redbook, Good Housekeeping, Home Beautiful, YM,* rarely concentrating on one article but zooming through the pages, synthesizing new window treatments, eyebrow design, the latest on Oprah. When I asked if she preferred one magazine to another, she said no, although she liked ones based on home life. Decorating, she said, was her special interest, but she would read anything as long as it wasn't sports. She cut out recipes mostly, she told me, but had only made two or three dishes straight out of the magazines. "I know what my girlfriends like to cook, so I give them the recipes."

When I had a Bud in front of me, I asked in sotto voce if anyone would mind if I checked to see if the football game was on. No one minded. Sharon handed me the remote control. I flicked through the stations and found the game. It didn't seem as interesting now that I sat in the bar. The sunlight outside seemed cordial and I missed it. Besides, it is always hard to know how many beers to drink in the middle of the day. Drink too few and you find yourself groggy and ready to sleep at four in the afternoon. Drink too many and you are headed into a long evening.

After my third beer, Sharon started asking me questions. She wondered where I was from, what I was doing in Ashton, what I did back home. From New Hampshire, she marveled. She told me it had always been her impression that people from back East worked harder than people in the West. As a rule, she said. Industrious. While she talked to me, she continued to flip pages. She seldom looked up. Now and then she stood and went to the rear of the bar where a series of doors apparently connected to her living quarters. Standing in the doorway, she had conversations with a male. Then she turned around and returned to the bar.

"His ex is coming," she told me after one of her conversations with the voice, "and she's a first-class bitch."

"Whose ex?" I asked.

"His," she said and wagged her head to indicate the back of the bar. "Guy's. I live with Guy."

"And his ex is coming here?"

She nodded and lit a cigarette. It turned out that the local boys' football team had won an important game somewhere to the south. Tough little bastards, Sharon said about the team. Not talented, but tough. Guy's son played on the team. Guy's ex was bringing the boy back from the game and Sharon said it was likely that she, the ex, would stay and have a few drinks.

"Which I wouldn't mind," Sharon concluded, "if she wasn't such a bitch. Wait until Kathy sees her."

"Who is Kathy?" I asked, trying to keep it straight.

"She's the nighttime bartender. She's wild. She's the leg wrestling champion of these parts."

"Leg wrestling?"

"You know, when you lay down and hook legs. She'll beat anyone."

Actually, I believed I was pretty good at leg wrestling. It had always been one of my covert talents. Growing up in a family of seven, leg wrestling had been one of many contests in our heathen childhood. Legs snapping like alligator jaws, we had laid on the living room floor through rainy afternoons, brother versus sister, sister versus sister, delighting when we could flip our opponent. Listening to Sharon go on about Kathy's leg wrestling ability, I felt—to use a western phrase— that I had the drop on the unsuspecting Kathy. Challenged to a leg wrestling contest, what would she see? A gentlemanly middle-aged guy, a fly fisherman, a vacationer. I didn't doubt she would take someone from New Hampshire less seriously than she would take a Texan or a Wyoming cowboy. I felt that the manhood of New England had been challenged.

At the same time, I wondered if I should anticipate gunplay when Guy's nameless ex returned to her ancestral watering hole. Meanwhile I watched the football game. At halftime I started out to walk Nellie, informing Sharon I would return.

I took Nellie for a walk to a tired potato field. The crop was already in, the ground turned for winter. I walked her along the patchy grass at the side of the road. When she finished her business, I let her off her lead for a while. It only took her a moment to find the first potato. She dug it up in a long furrow at the center of the field. I knew she was delighted. She lifted the potato in her mouth, an earthy tennis ball, and began prancing the way she does when something pleases her. She lifted her legs high and eyed me from sideways glances, her posture telling me she wasn't sure what I would think. Then, suddenly, she spotted another potato. They were leftover potatoes, ones too pulpy to harvest. She was shocked to find such abundance. She can mouth three tennis balls, but this was a different story. Instead of three or four, there were a hundred such potatoes scattered about. She spread her front legs and got another potato off the ground. Then she dropped one, picked another up, and so on. I could tell it drove her crazy. I told her to get them, to bring them to me, which only drove her nuttier. Her tail wagged in white arcs, wagged as it does only when she is completely involved in things. She finally managed to cram three potatoes in her mouth, but she couldn't make it back to where I was before dropping them. Her muzzle became coated with dirt. Her cheeks bulged with the potatoes, and her paws grew brown socks of earth and loose soil.

"Come on, girl," I called at last.

She came, but not before trying one last time to grab the potatoes again. They wouldn't cooperate. Unlike tennis balls, the potatoes simply grew more slick the more she mouthed them. She became less successful with each new try. Finally I had to walk into the field and put her on lead. I knew she would not willingly fail to retrieve. Retrieving was at the core of her nature. She would have remained in the field most of the night trying to bring potatoes to me.

I consoled her on the walk back to the truck, telling her we all have such days, then fed and watered her. I told her to lay down on her dog bed and she did. One of the benefits of traveling with a dog in autumn is that you don't have to worry about the truck getting too hot. She was as comfortable in the back of the truck as she would be in my living room at home. As I left her she was busy licking her paws, her mouth muddy with potato muck.

Kathy stood behind the bar when I returned. I'm not sure what I expected—maybe Calamity Jane or Annie Oakley—but

Kathy resembled a hairdresser from New Jersey. She wore an inch of makeup and her hair crept down her neck like black ivy. She smoked constantly, often with two going at the same time on either end of the bar. The cigarettes had turned her voice into something lovely, a hollow, gravelly sound like a garden hose spilling into an aluminum watering can. And she had a great laugh. It was a loud, raucous thing, a bark to start and a tapering semi-truck air brake at the end. She ran a lively bar.

I was prepared to be coaxed into the leg wrestling match, but not to be assaulted as soon as I returned to the bar. Apparently Sharon had told Kathy about me, letting her know that I was skeptical of Kathy's fabled ability. Kathy, to use western lingo, was spoiling for a fight. Sizing her up, I thought my chances were pretty good. I had five inches on her at least and unquestionably a good fifty pounds. Barring some trick that I didn't know about, I thought I'd beat her. Additionally, I was mindful of the comparative emptiness of the bar. I didn't relish the idea of laying down and wrestling with Kathy in front of an audience. It would be humiliating enough to simply lose; to lose in front of a group of braying men that would assemble later, to be flipped over like a hedgehog and regard the world through my legs, was more insult than I cared to contemplate.

Kathy came around the bar.

"Come on then," she said. "Don't say you weren't warned."

I mumbled something about not really wanting to wrestle, but she stretched out on the cigarette butts and told me she was ready. Shrugging, I laid down next to her. Guy, currently Sharon's boyfriend, came out of the back room to officiate. Sharon watched from a bar stool, shaking her head at me. Kathy hooked my arm along hers. I wondered again if there wasn't some trick I had already missed. Before I could get settled, Guy started counting.

On three Kathy's leg tucked in against mine. Vital, with the peristaltic strength of a constrictor, she began to fold me backwards. I kept expecting some gimmick to appear, but instead it was merely the unconquerable strength of the woman. Her ability, I guessed as she rocked me slowly backwards, came from years of sitting on a horse, her legs clamped like calipers around the hay-filled guts of a bay mare.

I don't think she won, but I'm certain I didn't. We slid a bit to the side—maybe I pushed—and the war ended. Kathy stood immediately and declared herself the champion, which was fine by me. Guy decided he should buy me a beer and Sharon went back to her magazines. I sat beneath the TV and watched the rest of the game, but I had already decided it was time to move on. Something about the afternoon had changed my blood. As I sat at the bar, I started to feel lonely and began to think of home again. I couldn't put a finger on why it happened. That evening when I stepped outside the air felt crisper, winter closer. I told Nellie it was last walk and gave her a biscuit when she finished her work. Then we climbed in the truck and headed back to the campground. She stretched out on the truck seat and put her head in my lap. Her chin stayed on my thigh, but her eyebrows danced at any sound I made. I tickled her paws and rubbed her back. I wondered if she was home missing too.

THE SUN RIVER

7:

ON MY WAY TO THE SUN RIVER, Montana, I stopped to fish for the afternoon at Wade Lake. I had heard about Wade Lake because the record for Montana trout came out of Wade Lake. The easterner who had told me couldn't remember whether it was rainbow or cutthroat or brookie, but driving up through the sage hills, with pronghorn antelopes as common as cows, it didn't seem to matter much. I knew the fish were likely to be large. My fear was that at this time of year they might stay down, their blood slowing to a turtle life just above the mud.

I have always been partial to lakes and ponds. While fly-fishing is perhaps best suited to moving water, I have an abiding affection for late summer evenings and rising trout on still water. For me nothing quite matches the pleasure of fishing to circles, the telltale marks of feeding trout. I love casting to a rise, watching the fly settle, then feeling the quick, greedy take of a large brookie.

Wade Lake is set in a bowl of mountains to the north and west of Yellowstone, not far off Route 287. It is located in the

Hidden Lake chain of lakes in the Beaverhead–Deerlodge National Forest. The surrounding land is serviceable cattle country and I passed six or seven livestock grates as I made my way up and over the surrounding hills. The lake seemed to be in hiding, thus the name Hidden Lakes, because the land leading to it revealed little promise of water. In fact, I stopped once or twice to reconnoiter, wondering if I had taken a wrong turn. But then the road deepened, became more established, and a wooden sign said Wade Lake with an arrow pointing the way I had thought it should point.

It took thirty minutes to descend, and in that time the landscape changed to what one would expect to find near a mountain lake. Pines marched up from the water to meet me. The grasses ripened. Starlings and swifts banked near the shoreline. Little by little I made my way to a campground near the center of the lakeshore and found a boat launching ramp. The campground appeared nearly empty and as I climbed into my gear I saw that snow topped the highest peaks. Trout season, at least in the higher elevations, was nearly finished.

Before climbing into my float tube I walked Nellie next to the lake. She waded in and out of the water, happy to drink her fill, happy to inspect the shoreline. We walked a half mile under the pines. She moved beautifully, her coat fully restored, her stride excellent. She nosed the pinecones and scouted for scents leading to the water. I followed her, letting her go where she liked. In the time we have known each other, she has never run away, never gone off in an unpredictable manner. I liked following her. She took her time and smelled everything. When she determined there were no new smells to discover, she began wading in the lake, looking for sticks to fetch. I threw a section of a pine branch as far as my arm could launch it and she swam after it. She fetched it seven or eight times. Though I had never taught her to give first, then shake off, she performed properly for a retriever. Hunters prefer the duck to be handed to them before the dog shakes, a trait Nellie had learned or received by luck or heritage. When we finished she carried the large stick back to the truck, the tip of one end nearly dragging on the ground.

I combed her out on the tailgate of the truck, gave her a biscuit or two, then locked her in the truck. I promised that I would not be long. She curled up on her dog bed and went to sleep.

As I backed into the water, the float tube suspended at my waist, I suddenly realized I didn't care about fishing that day. The same thing had happened once or twice before, but I still had no explanation for it. If I hadn't driven so far to get to Wade Lake, I would have marched out of the water and called it a day. The water seemed foreign to me; I had no clue where to begin, or how to start fishing. I saw no rises. The lake seemed vast and the prospects of catching a trout or two so dim as to be nearly unthinkable. A wind began blowing, too, taking the tops of waves and rinsing them white. The wind pushed my first few casts sideways, turning the large loops of my sinking line into quick roller coasters that tried to snap at the end. Nonetheless, I kept on.

I knew I had to get into a quiet cove, someplace sheltered, but propelling myself against the wind proved difficult. I kept casting, although it was merely throwing the line into the water and tugging it back. Chuck and chance. I felt no rhythm or cadence to anything I did. The large Matuka streamer on the end of my line caught the wind and fluttered like a luffing sail.

I would have felt more hopeful if I had seen someone else catch a trout, but the lake was empty as far as I could see. I told myself I would fish for five minutes more. Then three. I was ready to give up when I looked down and saw a huge trout following my retrieve, its nose inches from the retreating streamer.

I tried to keep the retrieve steady, luring the fish closer, but at the same time I was running out of line. To compensate I held the rod tip high and spun slowly, leading the trout like a show pony in a circle around me. I increased the speed of the fly, slowed it, then increased it again. Often slowing a retrieve, then hurrying it, will induce a trout to strike, but this one seemed happy to follow the Matuka in a circle with me absurdly performing pirouettes in the middle of a Montana lake.

I made four turns with the trout following. On the last one I stopped the streamer altogether. The fish sank below and I thought I had lost him. But as soon as I began to circle again, the trout fell into position behind the fly. Apparently it had no concern for my legs or swirling flippers. I began to find the situation wonderfully goofy. I hoped that a second trout, seeing the first one closing in on a minnow, might swoop in and steal the bacon, but after another turn or two that possibility faded.

It was a splendid predicament. Did it make sense to let the fish continue to follow? Or should I yank the streamer away and cast to unseen fish? To complicate matters, the trout appeared to be enormous. It's hard to judge the size of a fish underwater, but I was confident this one went over twenty inches.

Finally the trout made the decision for me. It did not swim away, but seemed to sink, sliding through the water in a crocodile glide that draped the darker currents over its back. I jigged with the streamer, reduced to party boat maneuvers, but the fish had disappeared.

I had never experienced anything like it. I didn't move for a minute or so, trying to figure out if I could have done anything differently. The fish was going to haunt me. I considered ways that I might cast to bring the fish back, to make it bite, to close the exchange we had between us, but there was nothing I could think to do.

For a while longer, I cast blindly, hoping for another trout, but gave up eventually. With the wind blowing more and more steadily, the water became an opaque disk. It occurred to me that a fish might be following my streamer on any cast, that strange chase taking place in the dark depths of the lake, but whatever had brought the trout to me seemed gone. After another hour, I kicked for shore.

To get my blood pumping again, I walked Nellie to an open field I had seen as I entered the campground and threw the Frisbee for her. She is a good Frisbee player and can leave the ground, leaping and twisting in one fluid motion to snap a Frisbee from the air. I threw ten times. It was an old game for us. I had kept a standing record of best-out-of-ten throws, the all-time top mark being eight. On this evening we came away with six, which wasn't bad given the uneven terrain. When we finished, I pretended to ignore her and walked away with the Frisbee dangling at my side. It was a game we had worked out years ago. Nellie snuck up and grabbed the Frisbee and it was my job to tell her she was a terrible girl, a bad dog, all the while playing tug of war with her. She growled and made a big deal of trying to get the Frisbee. When I let her win, she tried to push the Frisbee back in my hand to continue the war.

We drove back over the same road. Dust rooster-tailed behind us. Nellie pressed her nose to the windshield a hundred times. In Ennis, a town located in the heart of fly-fishing country, we stopped for food. I ordered us each a turkey sandwich. We ate it on the tailgate of my truck, overlooking the Madison

River. Once I had fished the Madison in the middle of the salmon fly hatch, a hatch which brings enormous insects onto the stream, each one as large as a chrysanthemum. The salmon fly hatch is a famous event in Montana—like the cherry blossoms in Washington or the wash of autumn colors in New Hampshire—and people come from around the world to fish it. The hatch occurs in a brief period, three or four days to a week, and no one can predict exactly when it will happen. I had blundered into it and had a wonderful time fishing with large, ropy flies, the trout glutted on such abundance.

That's what I thought about as we ate. When we finished, we drove in the twilight, Nellie's chin resting on my lap. I kept my hand on her and gave her a long rub. We listened to country music and left the windows down and the heat blasting. We headed north to the Sun River.

During the fall a few years ago I came close to being attacked by a black bear in New Hampshire. It was somewhat ironic, too, because I had returned from an Alaskan fishing trip a few weeks before and had happily related bear stories to anyone who wanted to hear them. Grabbing a listener, I informed her or him that it was astonishing how quickly one became accustomed to the presence of a bear. I explained how, on the salmon runs in Alaska, one couldn't escape contact with a bear. To prove my point, I related the story of a fly-in trip I had taken across the Cook Inlet. I had been dropped at the mouth of a salmon river and had cast merrily for coho through most of the morning. It had been a gray, rainy day, but the fish jumped madly, huge salmon the length of shotgun barrels crashing into the water. I used a Korean plastic streamer and was having marvelous luck when a guide in a skiff about thirty yards away whistled to me, pointed over my shoulder, then mouthed the word, Bear.

Up until that point, I had never seen a bear in the wild, never stood on the ground where a bear could easily grab me. My first impression on seeing the brown—a huge, adolescent male—was incredulity. The bear did not appear genuine. It resembled, instead, a George Lucas invention, a Wookiee or Ewok sprung mechanically to life. It came down a narrow waterfall, picking its way slowly, disturbed but not unnerved by my presence. It wanted the salmon, obviously, and it shook its wide head—its incredibly wide head—and grunted its displeasure. It wanted me out of its way. Unfortunately, Alaskan rivers are typically glacial, which means the bottom is often silted with several feet of muck. Moving quickly in them is out of the question, because you peg hold with each step. To oblige the bear, I began crab-walking to one side, leaving the bear easy access to the spot I had maintained for most of the morning. The bear lumbered down and patrolled the shoreline, eventually settling on the entrails of fish that had been cleaned earlier in the day. It pulled the entrails apart like gutty spaghetti, its head snapping up as the flesh gave way.

Amazingly, the bear became part of the landscape exactly as people had predicted. The guide boat had picked me up, but later I asked to be put ashore. I began fishing again, happy to be back on my feet, not particularly nervous when the bear went up the waterfall behind my back or disappeared for a moment on the white rocks that mounted in a cliff to my left. I kept fishing. Other fishermen joined me and we laughed anxiously when the bear came closer, shouting that we hoped the bear liked his meat well peppered, because the spray at our belts was going to be the only seasoning available.

Eventually the adolescent male left, only to be replaced by a female and a cub. Immediately the fishing guides in the skiffs told us to board. I understood the difference. The male had an aspect of tomfoolery, but the female was all business. She came down the waterfall in a quick, precise cadence, her single cub trailing her. Without a word from the guides, we hustled to be in the boats. I was the last one aboard. The female came into the water after me, not charging, but merely sealing the beach off so that there would be no dispute. She came into the water to her chest, then went up on her rear legs to scrutinize us. Her claws, I remember, resembled white bananas.

Later on that same trip, I watched a grizzly feed on a moose carcass in Denali, but again it was a comfortable situation. She saw me; I saw her. The grizzly remained on the carcass, indolent, bored, the moose hide spread beneath it like a rug. A ranger told me afterward that the bear had been on the carcass for a week. What I had witnessed was a well-fed bear a month or two free of hibernation.

With such experiences fresh in mind, I should have been prepared when I encountered the black bear. It was autumn in New Hampshire, the best season for walking. I had driven up to the town hall in Bridgewater, a splendid white building placed on a dirt road not far from the top of a mountain. Nellie hopped out in front of me. I also had a black Lab with me, a young female named Devil Dog, who belonged to an eight-year-old friend of mine. Both dogs took off down the dirt path, happy to be out on a beautiful fall afternoon. The sugar maples had already turned yellow and red newts dotted the dirt road as we walked into the woods. The temperature held in the forties.

The mosquitoes were finished for another year. It was the kind of day that makes life in New England get into your blood— a pumpkin forest on a black cat day.

We walked for thirty minutes before we came to bear scat— at least I thought it was bear scat. I called the dogs closer. Devil Dog is a timid, shy girl, a smallish black Lab who flunked out of the Guiding Eyes program because loud noises make her run for the hills. She came close at once, docile and obedient. Nellie, on the other hand, grudgingly swung by, then continued scouting the path on either side. She particularly liked the old stone walls where the chipmunks chattered at her from safety. I raised my voice a little and told her to be serious.

We continued on, but I was alert. After another fifty yards I heard a grunt and saw the wands of a berry patch rattling. I spoke to Nellie sharply and got her to come to me just as the bear broke free of the berry patch. Devil Dog cowered at my feet, but Nellie saw the bear at the same time as I did and strained to get at it. Luckily I had grabbed her collar in time. The bear—so black as to be nearly indistinguishable from the earth around it—charged directly at us. "Hey," I yelled but the bear continued coming. A second bear shot out from behind the first, going uphill and directly away from us. It was a cub, I realized. Then a third bear followed it, a second cub, while the mother bear kept coming at us. I suspected, watching it, that the female thought Devil Dog was one of its cubs. I also debated, in that intense moment, whether I would let the dogs go at it if it came down to them or me. Nellie, at least, would distract the bear while I made a getaway. It was a terrible, cowardly thought, but I also realized I couldn't defend Nellie anyway, and that Devil Dog was ready to join the Foreign Legion.

The female came within ten feet of us, made a sharp turn to the left, then crashed up the hill after the two cubs. Nellie choked against the collar. Devil Dog began barking at last, wandering within a three feet circle of me and making phony woof sounds, occasionally digging up the ground with her back paws. Although it sounds like a cliche, the hair on my neck had raised. I had always thought that was a convention of weak horror novels, but it turned out to be true. The bear, I estimated, had weighed about three hundred pounds. I heard it crashing up the hill for minutes afterward, its wide feet stirring the autumn leaves.

I thought of that black bear—and of bears in general—on the Sun River in Augusta, Montana, a day after I left Idaho and Wade Lake. On the first day of fishing the Sun River, I heard a cough in the bushes to the left of the river and suspected it was a bear. Anglers lie if they say they don't often worry about bears, but perhaps my antenna was pricked because the motel keeper in Augusta, where I had taken a room, had said the Sun provided prime berry forage for bears. I was up to my knees in water when I heard the cough. Fortunately Nellie was beside me and not scouting the bushes as she often does. We had only been fishing an hour. I had already landed three or four fair-sized cutthroat, all taking a Royal Coachman. As soon as I heard the cough I grabbed Nellie. I tried to listen, but it was difficult to distinguish sounds from the center of the stream. In a second or two I had persuaded myself that the noise might have been my imagination. It might also have been a steer foundered in the bushes. Either way, I waded downstream and away, fishing the pockets, pleased with the nimble tumble of trout from behind rocks. I told Nellie to heel and she did. We fished the rest of the morning without hearing more bear coughs.

The Sun River is nothing special, which is exactly why I like it. It is not a blue-ribbon stream. It is not a place where one is likely to run into five or six men in waders yelling about hatches. It's a river that spatters knee-deep for miles, has several wonderful runs where trout always hide, and has a million basketball-sized stones where trout linger and dodge out for passing flies. It connects the Rockies to the Missouri River in an easterly run. On this day in early October, I had the river to myself. I decided to believe that I hadn't heard a bear.

At lunch Nellie and I sat on the tailgate of my truck and did nothing for a time except bake in the bright October light. The night before I had taken out maps and calendars and gauged where we could go in the time left for the trip. We had another week, ten days at the most, if I drove back quickly. I wanted to make these final days on the road with Nellie count.

After I ate, I stretched out in the cricket grass of an open meadow and got Nellie to lay next to me. She was wet, but warm, and she rested beside me, her fur taking on heat, her body blocking the wind. When I had things arranged to my liking, I opened up *A River Runs Through It* by Norman Maclean. I did it cautiously, as I always do. It has been twenty years, almost exactly, since the book was first published. By a lucky set of circumstances, I had read it then, when I was twenty-two. I was enormously hungry for books at the time, gobbling up bestsellers as well as classics. At that young age, I loved books that represented writers at an equally young age—Hemingway's *The Sun Also Rises* or Fitzgerald's *This Side of Paradise*. In the same year that *A River Runs Through It* was published, I headed to

Paris, then to Africa, two years away from the publication of my own first novel.

Norman Maclean was not a young writer. He wrote the book shortly after retirement. It was as if his entire life had been distilled and dropped, page by page, into this one exquisite book. When the movie came out, complete with Brad Pitt in woolen trousers, I could not bring myself to see it. I still have not seen it, although as happens in modern America, enough of the movie soaked through promos and clips so that I feel as though I have. The novel is only marginally about fly-fishing; it is really about love and truth, about our inability to save what is near to us, about our obligations to our brothers. In the novel fishing is a means of transcendence.

I have never read the book straight through a second time. I have been too afraid to attempt it for fear it would disappoint me, but I frequently read and reread my favorite passages as I did that afternoon beside the Sun River.

Ted Taigen, my friend of thirty years, had first recommended *A River Runs Through It* to me. Ted and I had been friends since little league baseball when we both played for the Red Legs in Westfield, New Jersey. We had our first beer together when we were fourteen. When we were fifteen, we lied to our parents about where we were going and hitchhiked to the Jersey shore, where we slept under an old wooden rowboat, cold, damp, and feeling alive. We remained close friends into high school until his family moved to Colorado.

After my freshman year at college, I borrowed one hundred dollars from my father, told him I'd be back for school in the fall, and stuck out my thumb on Route 22 going west. If an eighteen-year-old came to me today and asked to do the same thing, I'd tell him he was crazy. But the early seventies were different times, and I was the kind of kid who wanted to go, to go anywhere, to get out of town. There was only one other person I could count on to share that feeling and I went that summer to visit him.

It was Ted who introduced me to fly-fishing. Tall and thin, with bright blue eyes and a remarkably retentive mind, Ted spent his summers hiking in the Rockies, visiting beaver ponds with his dog Patches, and learning to cast to bright-colored cut-throats and rainbows. After my experience on Mindowaskin Pond as a boy, I had not fished for fifteen years. When I arrived in Fort Collins, Colorado, Ted, who was a good student—and who would go on to become a professor of environmental studies at the University of Connecticut—hadn't finished his classes at Colorado State University. I was Huck Finn calling him away, but he had the good sense to lend me a tent, a fishing pole, and to send me off to the Poudre River, where I could camp for a while and wait for him to get free. I set up his old canvas tent next to the Poudre, ate beans and franks until they nearly killed me, and settled down with books at night. I climbed a mountain in sneakers and saw eagles and western pines for the first time, and in the early morning of the second day stabbed a salmon egg on a hook and let it swing through the riffles of the Poudre. The first fish I caught in my life was a trout in the Poudre River of Colorado, the fish hooking me as surely as I hooked it.

In memory I have linked that river to *A River Runs Through It*. All the conversations Ted and I have had, beginning when we were curious, adventurous, and young, were caught in the river along with the words of Norman Maclean. Ted and I still go fishing today. Each spring we visit the Rangeley Lake area of Maine and fish a river we know there. Our gear is better now and our wallets more full, but the river is still tied up in it some-how. We are younger when we stand next to the river.

In the motel room that night I made Nellie stand on the bed while I maneuvered a gooseneck lamp into position to examine her. I started by giving her a beauty shop, combing the feathers at the tops of her legs and gradually working the fur clean of burrs and sticks. She grunted in satisfaction at the brush strokes. When I finished, I made her down-stay on the bed and then rolled her onto her back. She lay for awhile with her paws flexed and droopy, prepared not for an inspection, but for a belly rub.

I didn't find much. The three or four bumps I came across might have been anything. She didn't react when I felt them to establish their dimensions. She lay upside down looking at me, her mouth in the funny curl dogs get when viewed from above. I couldn't help thinking she found the entire process humorous. Again, there was little to be done. I rubbed her belly for awhile, considered my options, then resolved to worry less. Before I let her go, I asked her if she was having a good time. She sneezed and got to her feet. I gave her a long last walk.

The next day we hit the water at ten. By midday the sun lay smeared on the water and each rivulet brightened the stones beneath it. I fished exclusively with dry flies, my baseline the Royal Coachman I had employed the day before, but also switching to a Dark Hendrickson and a hair-bodied Irresistible. Each of the flies proved effective. I fished well, which is to say, I fished patiently. The Sun is wide and friendly and I back cast with no fear of hanging up in the bushes, then feathered the fly down near various boulders, expectant and not often disappointed. Nellie stayed beside me, moving when I moved, her chin often against my knee. Each time I hooked a fish she inched forward, partially afraid, it seemed, partially stimulated to retrieve. Near lunch she began to tremble from the cold, so I called her and we repeated the process of the day before, resting in the bright sun until our bones felt heated again.

After lunch I rigged up my cane fly rod, the first fly rod I owned. I got it at a yard sale in Providence, Rhode Island, finding it amid a jumble of jigsaw puzzles and ashtrays. When I removed the rod from the cloth sack that it came in, the young woman running the sale came over and said the fly rod had been her father's. She said she had offered it to all the men in the family, but no one was a fisherman. She said she didn't necessarily want to sell it, but if I promised to use it, and to care for it, she would give it to me. I didn't quite know how to take her offer at first. Give it to me? I asked. She said yes. She said she wouldn't feel right selling it, because it meant a great deal to her father. But she said she would give it away to someone who would value it, which I found a marvelous distinction to draw.

I promised to care for the rod and I meant it. She must have seen the glimmer in my eye, because she gave me the rod. I bought a set of plastic ice trays out of a sense of obligation, then carried the fly rod home. I assembled the rod on the kitchen table, struck by how beautifully it fit together. The silver ferrules glided together smoothly. It was a three-piece rod, complete with a spare tip. When I flexed it, the entire rod shivered.

It was this rod that I assembled on the banks of the Sun River. I had long known that the rod was not worth a great deal. Several sporting goods dealers had reminded me that before the advent of fiberglass and graphite, cane fly rods were as common as Chevrolets. My fly rod possessed no brand name that anyone could identify, though one dealer guessed that it might have been a Fenwick. A Chevy was all right with me.

I strung it with a five-weight line, then carried it back to the water. It was a creaky old thing. The action, when I back cast, felt much stiffer than my graphite L.L. Bean rod. The cane rod probably could have carried an eight- or nine-weight line, but the cane had dried and I worried it might snap if I pushed it too hard. I fished carefully, enjoying the old-fashioned whip of the cane. Trout still rose to the flies. Nellie still followed. It wasn't the newest and best rod, but it felt comforting, like driving an old car on a country road.

During the course of the day I caught a few fish and spooked many more. They flashed from their hiding places near the rocks and ghosted across the water, amazingly rapid in their disappearance. Rainbow trout are not as fast as the common goldfish. One researcher posited that trout swim at a maximum speed of 440 centimeters a second, which can be translated to about 8.22 miles per hour. Salmon move faster, a fact to which I can attest.

On the Russian River in Alaska, I had hiked into a waterfall in the strange twilight of the equinox. I had never experienced daylight for a solid twenty-four hours and when I reached the falls, the moon was up and the sun still gave enough light for me to assemble my fly rod and to string a large streamer onto a thick tippet. On my first cast I hooked into a huge salmon (every cast brought a salmon, most of them foul hooked because they were so thick across the streambed) and it broke me off immediately. On the next cast I was ready. The salmon took off downstream in an incredible burst, its red body shooting out of the water like a fire hydrant, and I could do little except run after it. From M.R. Montgomery's book, *The Way of the Trout*, I have since learned that salmon swim approximately twice as fast as trout, reaching speeds of 800 centimeters a second or eighteen miles an hour. That is roughly the speed maintained by a well-conditioned sprinter in a 440-yard dash on a flat track. I scrambled after the red salmon on the Russian River in Alaska. It escorted me down to a second pool, then broke me off again, this time the line snapping back in a slingshot toward me. I never did land a red salmon, admitting finally that they could outrun me.

I took Nellie on a last walk before we went to bed. We walked down the paved road that fronted the motel, then I let her go to investigate a patch of grass. She was lazy and docile, tired from a day wading in the water. A few snowflakes began to fall. When she came back to me, I put her on the leash again and waited awhile in the darkness. You could see a long way. Snowflakes pulled each other down out of the sky like white spiders dipping softly onto grass.

We walked back to the motel. The front desk had already closed. There would be no more customers that day. As I passed down the hall to my room, I heard one TV after another, each with a different voice yet all oddly the same. When I unhooked Nellie's leash inside the room, she put her nose on the edge of the bed, asking permission to get up. I told her to go ahead, but not to hog the whole thing. She curled at the foot of the bed, tail to nose. I sat beside her and gave her a rub. In a little while she began to snore. I read for awhile, then turned out the light.

THE BIGHORN 8: RIVER

I REACHED THE BIGHORN RIVER on this, my second visit to the Crow Reservation, on October tenth, a day known as Dog Whipping Day in certain parts of ancient England. The day has an interesting derivation. When monasteries flourished in England, the monks gave food and clothing to the poor at a fair on October eleventh. One year a dog stole a large piece of beef, and from that day any dog seen near the monastery on the eve of the fair received a whipping. The dog-whipper wore a special costume—pink velvet knee breeches, a blue coat with silver buttons, a cocked hat and white silk stockings. He carried a huge club and lazy tongs. The custom has long ago faded to obscurity, but as a dog fancier I cannot let the day go by without remembering its origins.

The Bighorn is as famous for rattlers as it is for trout and I kept an ear and eye cocked for snakes as I walked the shoreline. I am not a great fan of snakes. I have been forced to kill cobras—spitting and king cobras—and Gabon vipers while living in West Africa, but I never liked the worry one experiences in snake country when lifting bricks or lumber or stepping across a dried streambed. Unlike cobras or Gabon vipers, rattlers at least have the good manners to let you know they are nearby. Wearing waders as I made my way along the rocky shore of the Bighorn River, I worried more for Nellie than for myself. She had confronted rattlers before, and had shown good sense by backing away, but often she entered brush that seemed prime snake habitat. I tried to keep her close, but was only moderately successful. Fortunately it was fairly late in the season, I reasoned, and the snakes, if we came across any, might tend to be sluggish. Ideally I might have had a jacket similar to the ones made for bird dogs to slip onto Nellie. I would have settled for an orange blaze jacket, the type she wears during hunting season when we walk the woods behind my house, but I had forgotten even that protection. To fortify us both, I made as much noise as possible walking beside the river.

I had a specific spot in mind. Several miles downstream from Yellowtail Dam the water turned into a white frothy mix. I had largely ignored the rapids the first time I had fished the Bighorn, but two young fellows from Montana later told me that huge fish lay in the faster water. They happened to have their rigs in the back of their pickups and they spent a few minutes showing me how to set up the terminal tackle. It was a classic jig system, with a minuscule shrimp at the end of the line and a steel weight, fair sized, approximately two feet up the leader. With the tackle ready, you simply dabbed the fly different places in the white water, occasionally ferreting out a trout not more than a few feet from your legs. It did not make for particularly dignified fishing, but the white water had stayed in my mind for several years, titillating me with images of large fish waiting on a food line. On the first visit I had several extraordinary tugs, but had never actually landed a fish. Contrary to popular thought, nothing ensures an angler's return to the same water as a near miss. A lucky day can easily pass from memory, but a fish suggested, though not landed, is the finest bait to lure anglers.

Nellie became nervous when I prepared to enter the white water. She doesn't like me wading in deeper water, because then she can't accompany me. I told her to be still, to take a rest, and gave her a biscuit as a bribe. She chomped the biscuit readily enough, but wasn't satisfied with the arrangement. She waded with me until I reached my knees. I tried to sound stern when I told her to wait on shore, but she knew me too well to buy it.

Almost immediately I became absorbed in plunking the jig around the white water, although it was not easy wading. Water cut at my knees and rocked me this way and that. Each movement had to be calculated; each foothold felt borrowed. When I cast, or swung the jig out, it plunked into the water, then rattled along the bottom, hitting stones and various currents, reporting to my fingers the topography of the river bottom. Noise rose from the water and everything became liquid. Whatever it is that separates us from water began to dissolve.

Five minutes into the rapids I had my first strike, a short, violent tug that made me wonder if it had not simply been the shrimp snagging a boulder. I cast in the same spot and this time stood ready. The trout hit in rhythm, taking the shrimp in the exact position as it had the first time. The rod dipped like the hazel branch of a water dowser.

It was a large fish. I knew that immediately. It lunged downstream and picked up the weight of the rushing water, then it jumped free of everything and dangled for a moment in the

October light. When it fell back in the water it gathered the force of the rapids and surged away and cross stream, sawing my leader against rocks and white Vs of surface turbulence. I waded carefully to slower water and invited the fish to swing down and out of the rougher patches. It obliged me, though it made two runs back to the wilder water before I brought it to shore.

The span of one hand is almost exactly ten inches and this rainbow was not quite two spans. Nellie came close and nosed it. I let it go underwater and watched it gain its balance, then shoot off into the white water again. I tried to imagine what it must be like to live in such active water, how a trout can pick out a tiny shrimp in the turbulence, anticipate it, then maneuver to eat it. I wondered if it is a mistaken notion to think of the fish as separate from the water any more than protozoa floating in a turbidity current might be said to be separate from the hydrogen and oxygen atoms surrounding it. A trout may not live in water as we live in air. Perhaps the trout is closer to it, is involved in it, in ways we fail to comprehend. Perhaps a shrimp enters a trout as much as the trout consumes the shrimp. It is merely our perception of things that assumes a shrimp does not seek out the trout.

I fished for a good hour, dunking the weighted tackle here and there. It was more prospecting than fishing, but two more trout took, each almost precisely the size of the first. At noon I broke for lunch and sat on the bank with Nellie. I did not much like the land around the Bighorn. Cottonwood trees lined the banks, but they seemed untrustworthy trees. The river ran too bright and wet for the dry countryside around it. It is hard to fish the Bighorn, I realized, without being reminded that it was created by a dam. The river wanted to be a stream.

146

The Yellowtail Dam, constructed in 1965, turned an otherwise average river into one of the premier trout habitats in the world. Anglers debate over how many fish the Bighorn holds—with estimates rising as high as a million fish per mile—but there is no debate that it is a river rich with fish. The cold water released from the bottom of the dam, combined with the silt and vegetable matter on the streambed, makes for nearly perfect trout water. The Bighorn is a river, in short, that a trout might imagine for itself.

I had caught the largest trout of my career last time I was on the Bighorn, which was why I had included it when I drew up an itinerary for this trip. On that first trip, I had been fishing for several hours with pretty good results, but I hadn't tied into a large fish. To catch a number of fish is no miracle on the Bighorn. I caught the large trout a few minutes before rain covered the river. Storm clouds had threatened most of the day, but I had such good luck that I ignored the approaching storm and concentrated on the excellent dry-fly fishing. The fish volunteered for a red hackled fly of my design, an ugly thing that somehow matched what the trout favored that day. Nevertheless, I was conscious that the fish I caught tended to be ten to eleven inches. They were good fish, no doubt, but I had caught plenty of twelve-inch trout in the East. I felt eager to tie into something larger and felt somewhat cheated by trout that did not live up to their western reputations.

When I finally did hook a large fish, the moment was absurdly mythic. The entire sequence would have served Hollywood, because the threat of rain had long ago chased other

147

anglers from the river. I stood alone in America's richest trout water, the clouds ridiculously portent. The first rises of the large fish mixed with the splatters of the storm's beginning. The only thing that did not lend itself to a movie event was the fact that the trout did not rise in the center of the stream. It rose directly downstream from me in water no deeper than my knees. Casting to it required nothing showy. I simply plunked the fly in the water and let it swing down to an imaginary bib floating in front of the trout. The trout rolled and took the fly. I lifted my rod tip and waited.

Large trout are silent when they are hooked. Small fish dance immediately and though there is pleasure in the quickness of their responses, the silence before a big trout surges is ultimately more rewarding. When the trout at last began to move, my fingers were ready. The fish shot into the middle of the river, yanking line out and making my reel hum. At the same time the rain intensified and several distant drums of thunder clunked in the valley. The fish pulled. I scrambled down the shoreline and followed it. Rain splattered on the rocks and lifted the smell of sage and root dirt from nearby bushes. I played the fish lightly, letting it run whenever it liked. At times the fish jumped on the tail of a peal of thunder. Lightning wicked across the valley and the light became haunted.

I landed the trout in the shallows, kneeling next to it and letting it rest in the hammock of my fingers. I estimated it to be about twenty-six inches. It was a fat thing. When I released it, it knocked gravel aside as it squirted back into the stream. I can still hold my fingers apart, accurately I believe, to the exact dimension of the trout's passage against my hand.

I had caught that fish during the first visit I made to the Bighorn River several years before when I had volunteered for a childhood literacy program at Crow Agency, Montana, the tribal seat of the Crow Reservation. It had been an exceedingly difficult summer. The program for which I had volunteered suffered all the usual hardships. It had been underfunded, poorly organized, and viewed with suspicion by the Crow. I had lived in a tent behind a local minister's house, escaping during the free hours to fish the Bighorn. In time I had learned that the Bighorn Mountains are sacred to the Crow, that Yellowtail Dam, the large federal project that had transformed the river into a world class fishery, had the aura of a curse to the people who live beside the water.

The Crow had arrived only fifty or sixty years before Lewis and Clark. To put it in perspective, the Crow and Northern Cheyenne took the plains from the *gens des serpents*, their spear-carrying predecessors now known as the Snake Indians, after Columbus discovered Cuba. In an historically brief period, they drove the Snake Indians to the desert of the Great Basin and assumed the fertile grounds watered by the Bighorns. The horse culture relied on grass and it is not surprising that the Crow named their settlements accordingly: Lodge Grass, Rotten Grass. Even the Battle of the Little Bighorn is known to the Lakota and Cheyenne as the Battle of Greasy Grass.

The United States Government had once granted the Crow a reservation covering most of Wyoming and Montana, including all of Yellowstone, only to reclaim the land when western migration surged. The Crow also had, I believe, longstanding guilt at being one of the few nations never to have raised arms against the expanding European forces. In fact, the legacy of White-Man-Runs-Him, a famous Crow guide for Custer, is viewed with a mixture of admiration and embarrassment. The Lakota, who fought against the Crow relentlessly, view them as traitors as a result of the Crows' compact with white settlers. It is a thorny issue, one that brushes any person of European ancestry coming to the reservation.

The summer I worked on the reservation some Crow children stoned Nellie. A pack of twelve-year-old boys cornered her in a vacant lot and began pelting her with stones. She appeared stunned when I found her, astonished that people, from whom she expected kindness, could harm her. She had not turned vicious or even angry, but had actually leaped to catch some of the stones, thinking that surely they were tennis balls. Fortunately the boys had not done any serious injury. I yelled at them to leave her alone and they disappeared without protest. Nellie came to me with her tail down, as if she had done something wrong. I knelt next to her and pet her a long time. I never left her out of my sight again on the reservation.

Walking back to my truck at mid-afternoon, Nellie surprised a coyote. It happened so suddenly it caught me unawares. I had been thinking about snakes, naturally, but when Nellie dove into a thicket and a thin dog jumped out the other side, I was momentarily confused. I looked around for another angler— thinking he or she had brought a dog along—but then I heard Nellie's deep-throated growl, the one I had only heard two or three times in her life. A second later I understood. The coyote shot off perpendicular to the river and Nellie followed her for twenty yards. I shouted her name and luckily got her attention. The coyote disappeared, leaving only a wagging batch of river grass marking her retreat. Nellie came back to me, growling and bristled, the world safe for democracy once again.

Good girl, I told her. I told her that she was a fierce old thing. I told her I hoped I would be as fierce when I reached her age. She didn't stay quiet under my hand. She continued circling in front of me, coyote scent lingering in her nostrils. She sneezed and kept circling long past any reasonable period. After a while I told her to stop and to follow me back.

We slept that night at a small campground not far from the Fort Smith Ranger Station, although to call it a campground might be overstating the case. It was a ledge of dirt overlooking Montana 313. Someone had put a few fire rings to mark parking spaces, but those were the only amenities. Setting up for the night I was keenly aware of the trout trade: float boats rattled back and forth and large, four-wheel-drive vehicles with electric roll-down windows fluttered up and down the road, the interiors jammed with guys in neoprene. Most of this occurred at cocktail hour and I was conscious of how out of proportion the wealth of these anglers was compared to the host tribe members.

I cooked tomato soup for dinner and drank a beer while watching the sun set. A layer of dust clung to Nellie and I brushed her coat when the evening started to grow cooler. Afterward we sat on the tailgate and shared some crackers. I held the crackers and made her bite them in half, then again, then again, until the remaining piece was microscopic. Her mouth remained amazingly gentle. Each time she halved the half, her teeth worked to find a safe purchase. We ate five or six crackers that way.

Later that night, near two in the morning, Crow kids woke me. They circled my truck on four-wheelers, roaring around and having a hell of a time. Nellie growled each time a kid buzzed close. I knew, from my summer on the reservation, that parents seldom directly discipline their children, thinking instead that uncles and aunts should provide guidance while parents give only love. That system, like many things on the reservation, had broken down over the years and often now the kids went unchecked. Laying in the truck, attempting to ignore the racket, I tried to think of a reason kids should be up four-wheeling on a weekday night at two in the morning. I couldn't come up with one. Then I tried to arrange the few words of Crow I had in my vocabulary into a sentence, hopefully one that would tell them I needed to sleep and they needed to go home. All I could recall with any certainty was the word *showdagi,* a general greeting spoken by biting off the last syllable. I thought perhaps that might work to make them realize I knew a little about the reservation, but then I simply decided to wait it out.

They left around four. Apparently I had camped next to a good ramp or jump. The next morning I found tire tracks everywhere around the truck, most of them leading to a track above the campground. The treads left diagonal gouges in the dirt. At the top of the rise, where the trail connected to a second trail, the kids had apparently jumped repeatedly. The tread marks stopped and then started again after a span of six or seven feet. I looked to see a village or settlement along the second path, but the trail simply vanished in white, dusty land. It was a long way to travel, I thought, for a six-foot jump.

Once a summer, generally near the Fourth of July, my dad rented a party boat and took everyone from his New York office bluefishing off the New Jersey coast. As a boy I remember it as an important and exciting day. During the week leading up to the fishing trip, my mother cleaned the house and we made some effort to put the backyard in shape. A birch grove covered the rear half of our acre, and here we arranged a picnic table, a grill, a metal washbasin filled with ice for beer and soft drinks, and six or seven shaky lawn chairs. Under my father's eye, we raked the gardens that had suffered seven children running wild from one summer to the next.

My parents did not entertain well or easily. Entertaining takes the time neither of them possessed to perfect and accomplish with grace. As a result, the day of the bluefishing party carried with it a large but slightly uncomfortable air.

I was the youngest, not yet ten by the time this summer tradition had ceased, and therefore never got the chance to go fishing. The party boat—even the name thrilled me—existed as a mythical place. In bed the morning of the expedition, I heard the thunk of doors and cabinets, the early morning hush as my father and brothers stole out of the house. Most of the day was a long, hot wait for them to return, the boat, in my imagination, drifting on a sea filled with glimmering fish.

Finally the men returned. I recall nearly climbing out of my skin with excitement as I heard the cars and doors slam, the shouts, the masculine booms. Porky, still alive, went to greet them and bark, while I made my way to the front yard. There, yanking burlap bags of bluefish from the trunks of the car, the men clustered and laughed, continuing jokes that had started early that morning. I listened to hear who had been seasick, who had "high hook," who had the richest sunburn. The men talked a great deal about the boat pool, which I learned in time meant the wager, a dollar a head, paid as a jackpot for the largest fish.

I felt pleasure at seeing my father surrounded by men, happy, the host, carefree in a way he could not be around us. Standing beside the open car trunks, a sodden bag of bluefish in either hand, his office skin glowed red for a change. My mother and sisters and I were a new audience, and as we made our way to the backyard, one of the bags invariably ended up in my hands. The bag glittered with weight and water and it smelled, in every breeze that found it, of the sea and boats and distance.

My job, given partly to include me, consisted of dumping the fish on the green grass and hosing them down. Tilting the bag, letting the fish slide like coins onto the grass, the ring of adults around me, I reveled in my importance. I sprayed them the way my father had shown me: my thumb cocked in the open mouth of the hose, my wrist milking water from our house, the bluefish staring in open wonder at a world foreign to them. Porky nosed the fish, edging between the men's legs, while this or that person stepped forward and said he had caught this one, that one, the one over there.

Then it was time for drinks, more drinks, because the men had already begun on the boat, some of them getting loopy with sun and fresh air. I remember the men as being kind to me, wanting to include me because I had been left out of the more serious business. I carried beers around and later, when the sun went down, caught fireflies and cooked marshmallows on the grill. I handed a marshmallow to my dad at the end of one long boat day. His attention, fixed on something another man said, canted away from me. Mechanically his fingers squeezed the marshmallow from the stick in my hand, then he lifted the marshmallow toward his mouth. Something stopped him, though, and his eyes finally met mine. *Thank you*, he said, mouthing the word so as not to interrupt the other man. His hand lifted and rested on my shoulder, the smell of bluefish riding his skin.

154

I fished the Bighorn again directly beneath the dam, casting to rising fish with a small Adams and having pretty good luck. Nellie watched. It was a gray day and cold; had I been home in New Hampshire, I would have been satisfied to sit by a fire and read. But this was the Bighorn and one only has so many days beside a river like that in a lifetime. I had lately been flirting with the idea of including one last stop on my itinerary, but equally compelling was the idea of heading home. I had decided, sometime in the night, to let fate show me a sign, which is another way to say that if the fishing was good I would visit one more spot, the North Platte in Wyoming. I had never been to the Platte, but several people had told me that the fishing was superb. Still, I wasn't certain if I wanted to make the effort.

I had just released my fourth fish when I was joined by another angler, a bluff, rotund fellow who greeted Nellie as joyfully as she greeted him, then asked me if I knew the origin of Golden Retrievers. When I said I didn't think such things were exactly knowable, he recited a story that has been repeated so often it has gained the varnish of truth. He claimed to have had three Goldens in his day and had made it his business to look up their history.

The Golden Retriever, he contended, sprang from a cross between one of Lord Tweedmouth's sporting dogs, probably a spaniel named Belle, and a blonde retriever brought from a cobbler who named his dog Nous, meaning Wisdom. Tweedmouth, he supposed, was a potty Britisher, one of those mid-nineteenth-century eccentrics who had too much house and too much time on hand. He said that Tweedmouth cleverly bred the dog

155

to other spaniels and curly coated retrievers, eliciting qualities for which Goldens are now justly famed—a soft mouth, curly hair with a waterproof undercoat, and an exceedingly gentle disposition. Retrievers made excellent upland dogs—bird dogs, essentially—and of course wonderful water dogs. He said Tweedmouth bred the dog to sit beside a hunter all day in a boat, quiet and peaceful, only springing to action after the kill. At that point the dog was programmed, by instinct, to leap into frigid water not for a joy of swimming, but out of love for the hunter.

While the man remained petting Nellie, I told him the simple version of the origin I'd read and often repeated. Goldens were the product of an English spaniel and a cross made haphazardly when a pack of large white Russian circus dogs mated with the spaniel. The Russian imprint increased the spaniels' size and strength, nudging the breed to modern standards. I said I liked this history better. It left the Retrievers' origins as a matter of happenstance. I could tell, watching the angler, that he didn't appreciate my story. He had his version of things and was happy with it. He thanked me, gave Nellie one last rub, then headed off downstream. I had brought a thermos of coffee with me and I decided to take a break and watch the river. At times I am an impatient fisherman, choosing to enter the water before I have really studied the current and insect life. I have gotten better as I have gotten older—which means I have become more patient—and now take nearly as much pleasure in sitting beside a river as in fishing. I propped my rod against a sapling, then unscrewed the thermos cap and poured a cup. The heat was welcome. The air temperature was in the mid-forties, with clouds moving quickly across the sky. Nellie came to sit beside me. I dug a biscuit out of my pocket and gave her a treat. For a time we didn't do much but sit together.

I have determined two ways to watch a river. The first is performed with a conscious state of mind, the scientific approach that trout books and fishing diagrams champion. I have known any number of anglers who speak with pride of this or that fishing companion who does not cast until he has turned over stones, netted a few flies, dipped a thermometer into the water. When I first began fishing, I relied primarily on that method. I saw a river as a detective story, one that, if studied assiduously enough, could be unraveled. The reward, naturally, would be a large payoff in fish. The keener the detective, the luckier the angler.

Over the years, however, my approach has begun to change as a result of observations concerning my fishing performance, ones that do not fit precisely the scientific approach. For instance, I have often known when fish were about to hit not because I happened to tie on the correct fly, but because I understood somehow they were going to take. For lack of a better word, I have felt glimmers of harmony, splendid moments when the fishing became not an uncertainty but a fixed, knowable outcome. Of course one mentions such things at one's peril, opening oneself up to jokes about Zen and karma and myriad cracks about consciousness, but most of us have felt such moments without having to name them. We hit a baseball with a clean, solid swipe that seemed nearly predestined. When it occurs, the bat does not so much resonate as confirm the knowledge in our arms and legs and blood. Basketball players know a shot was going in the moment it left their fingers. So it can be with fishing.

The implication of this knowledge, at least for me, is that my second approach to a river is to open myself to it. It is the reverse of the scientific approach. Instead of separating the river into parts, which is the inevitable outcome of the scientific approach, I try to see the river as a whole. Usually this method demands that I stop trying to distinguish, to pick apart, instead allowing my vision to soften and blur so that the river may volunteer parts of itself to be studied.

I tried it that day on the Bighorn with Nellie beside me. I had difficulty tuning out the empirical part of my mind that continued to ask what kind of flies hatched, what nymph matched what potential stone fly, what tippet I needed to clip back to. Little by little I had to let that nervous, demanding part of my intellect relax. It did so in stages, surging back to take command as quickly as I suppressed it. Gradually the periods where I could simply observe grew longer. My vision began to blur. I became conscious of the river running over rocks.

I did not *become the river* or approximate any of the silly jokes commonly floating around American pop culture. But I did become calmer. After a while, when I waded in and began fishing again, I caught a cutthroat on a cast that I felt certain would bring results. But I also had feathered the fly down nicely on the water, which may have been the reason the fish responded. Either way, the fish did not surprise me.

In my last hour on the Bighorn I caught three fish. The middle one was the largest. Nellie came into the shallows to inspect it. I knelt beside it and let it rest for a second in my fingers. Its gills beat with the lapping water. The sky reflected in the water around it. When it skittered back to the center of the river, it looked to pass among the clouds.

TON GUE RIVER

9:

WEST OF BURGESS JUNCTION, halfway between Cody and Sheridan, Wyoming, we stopped at the Tongue River. The Tongue is an easy river that meanders beside Alternate Route 14 in the Bighorn Mountains. I liked the river for Nellie because it runs at great elevation in a welcoming valley, a flickering line between cresting mountains. We had no worry about bears, or about snakes, or about severe drop-offs. Visibility ranged up to twenty miles in a spacious bowl, so that I could watch Nellie roam no matter how far away she cared to go. At the topmost peaks bighorn sheep and mountain goats picked their ways among the rocks. They were a rare sight, worth stopping to look for. Free-range cattle sometimes used the land, and occasionally elk herds grazed in the lee of an outcropping.

I knew, from an earlier trip, that the Tongue was a modest, kindly river, producing unlimited numbers of six-to-eight-inch cutthroats. In many ways the North Tongue was a classic western stream, with trout living suspicious lives in the shadows of willow bogs. The river was too high for beaver, or at least

I had never discovered any beaver activity, and so the river flowed as directed by gravity, the water glacial, the course always downhill.

I listened carefully to weather reports as we approached, and when the forecast called for a clear night, I decided to take Nellie on a short hike. We needed to get away from the truck. It was our last chance to sleep out at significant elevation — the Tongue River ran above ten thousand feet — and I reasoned the stars would be as close as they were likely to get.

We left the truck at three. Nellie wore her backpack containing food and mittens and I carried a lightweight pack with the bare necessities. She had the serious demeanor she always has when she wears a pack and knows she is carrying something important. We followed the Tongue River as it veered slightly from the road, heading north. I kept my fly rod strung and when we came to promising water, I cast a Pale Evening Dun to dark places. At the second hole, a wide washboard riffle that emptied into the skillet of black water, I caught ten fish in as many casts. The fish were small and aggressive, as lively as crickets. Nellie watched for awhile, then scouted ahead. The tinkle of her bear bells came over the sound of the water.

Three miles upriver, near a creek named Dry Gul, we established camp. I had brought the tent, knowing it would be cold, but I hadn't bothered with a camp stove. I set up the tent on a small rise, mountains everywhere around us. After we ate two peanut butter and jelly sandwiches each, Nellie patiently chewing when the peanut butter stuck to the roof of her mouth, we fished a productive hole directly below our camp. The trout fought to take the fly, though none was more than six inches. The fish continued to hit the fly even after it had been reduced to a few pale hackle feathers and a gnawed tinsel body. At that elevation, in such brisk water, the fish could not risk being selective.

Later, wind seemed to push the light away as the sun fell behind the mountaintops. Up to her shoulders in the river, Nellie felt the change, too. Her fur ruffled in the breeze and she looked to me several times when the wind blew the strongest. It was autumn now and fast becoming winter. We both felt it.

I put my fly rod up and found a comfortable spot to watch the stars come out. Nellie came to sit beside me. I scooted around and put my head on her back, using her for a headrest, but she didn't seem to mind. Cold air swept above us, yet near the ground it did not feel too bad. We watched the planets appear, then the stars. The sky grew darker until each star stood out, white against black against the gray of the mountaintops. Nellie remained stationary, only her nose sniffing into the wind. She did not budge for an hour, and by that time the stars had eaten into the blackness, shuddering white in a cold sky.

We went to bed early. I knew it was no use to try to keep her out of the sleeping bag, so I spread it and let her come underneath. Her heat was welcome. I read for awhile, then turned off the light and listened to the wind jiggle the tent. Nellie snored deep in the bag. The wind grew wilder until I fell asleep and stopped listening. I imagined it lifting us like a small orange kite, lofting us into the wind streams above the valley.

I woke several times during the night and woke for good before daylight. Nellie came out of the tent with me and drank from the stream in the rinsed darkness. The wind had subsided and I felt the pleasure of morning. The moon, a morning moon, stood in a crescent near the Cloud Peak Wilderness. I climbed up fifty yards above the tent and watched the sunlight come over the eastern edge of the Bighorns. Nellie found me and came to sit beside me. We didn't see any mountain goats or bighorn sheep, but we stayed where we were until light reached us. Fog puffed from the water currents and it was possible, looking closely, to believe the river breathed. We watched it until the sun cut into the mist and pushed the white webs down into the streambed, then we packed.

I fished the same pools going back. The trout cooperated again. At one bend in the river I hooked into a twelve-inch cutthroat, its size surprising me when it hit. It hurried to return to the cut bank where it had been hiding, but I guided it downstream until it let me release it. It disappeared before my fingers had completely uncurled. Watching it go, I told myself to remember the readiness of the trout at this elevation. I also told myself that too much of this success would spoil me for eastern fishing, where it was common to spend an entire day frothing the water for one fish. Still, I could not resist casting to such greedy trout. They destroyed two flies with their hungry mouths. Sometimes they hit the leader when it caught the light and glinted.

Near the last pool, I stretched out on my belly and stared at the water. Nellie crept up beside me, uncertain of what I was doing. I saw both our reflections in the water. We made a funny picture, man and dog staring intently at ourselves, our reflections stretched and bent according to the shimmer of stream water.

I looked for trout. I had read years before that one could catch trout with his hand if he was patient enough. I had also read that trout, hiding from predators, will stick their heads in the gravel bottom and linger in the current, tail up, ready to be grabbed. I could not easily imagine catching such quick, elusive creatures by hand, but it was worth a try. My polarized sunglasses permitted me to see the bottom of the stream, and in time the trout became visible, gray commas with speckled backs.

I knew trout were particularly wary of things approaching from above—birds being one of their primary predators—so I sank my hand and let it drift as loosely as possible, a phony clump of tissue moving quietly toward the trout. I did not manage to get close before the fish scattered, their bodies disappearing before I could say for certain I had seen them move. I decided, after such an obvious failure, simply to watch the trout instead. That plan worked better. My eyes peeking over the bank, I watched as the tiny cutthroat clustered at the head of the pool. They moved so quickly that it was difficult to see them unless they swam together, as they often did, when some new food source entered the water. They had only a moment before a larger cutthroat, one perhaps five inches long, zoomed in and took whatever escaped the little fish. It was impossible to see what they aimed to eat. Mostly they squirted from side to side, picking up dots of freshwater shrimp or stone flies. The smaller fish, according to the theory I developed, had the advantage of going first due to their body size. They could swim in shallow water, thereby getting the drop on whatever came into the pool. The larger fish had to wait. Sometimes the small trout moved not as animals, but seemingly as vegetation anchored to the bottom of the stream. As I stared, the fish became weeds and had to be transformed back to trout by conscious effort.

The larger fish, sometimes as long as six or seven inches, lingered at the back of the pool. They moved only for bigger meals. I knew, from experience, that they lived on a biological equation that matched the energy spent to retrieve a meal against the energy gained by consuming the meal. They could not work at a negative balance for long, obviously, which was why, in the spring, larger trout were particularly fond of minnows. The minnows, or dace, provided more calories, more sustenance, than stone flies or nymphs could possibly provide. Spring fishing with streamers that replicated minnows or smelt constituted an old tradition in Maine's cold lakes.

As I continued to stare at the water, I became aware of the life, and the suggestion of life, at the level of the banks and stream. Water striders flickered back and forth, and late insects, mostly mosquitoes, buzzed near the tired grasses. A weary bee landed on a log and lingered in the sun, its back leg sacks heavy with propolis. If it landed on the water, as it might easily do in its fatigue, the fish would have it in a blink. Underneath the stones, when I reached down and turned them, I found stone flies and hellgrammites, the scorpion-shaped insects trout love so much. Black crickets chiggered in the river grass, and above, like a blade moving on a strap, swallows and flycatchers came to skim the surface.

Resting so close to the water, I thought of myths about water nymphs, the small, magical creatures that come out in the evening and drift in the hazy summer air. It was possible to imagine them here, on the Tongue, drifting slowly as the water struck away from the mountaintops. I told Nellie that she should find a water sprite, and that made her stand and shake. She went off to scout out something new, and in time I went with her.

The last hole we fished was a large, deep spike of water that had been hammered between two towering boulders. I had missed the pool the first time, mistaking it in the dim light for nothing substantial. Now, in full sunlight, I saw that it was the equivalent of a fish cave, a dark musky place where larger trout could gather. It took a few moments to get into position to fish it. I decided to tie on a grasshopper, a black one, and let the fly hit the rock before plunking into the pool. I wanted the action to look as natural as possible. If I performed it correctly, I imagined the cricket would land with its fiddle legs crooked to gather its senses, its body bunching to hop free of the water. Trout could not resist. If nothing bit, then I doubted a fish lived in the hole.

Wobbling on two rocks, I cast in a long, loopy wave and succeeded in thudding the cricket into the right-hand boulder. The cricket stalled in flight and I quickly lifted the cigar butt of the rod up, allowing the fly to drop, not softly, into the water. I wanted commotion. The cricket performed beautifully and landed with a tiny plunking sound that I thought would summon the fish from below. Then I waited. The cricket glided across the hole, then darted into the white water below. Nothing had taken.

It was okay. I repeated the process. And again. I floated the same fly over the water twenty times, then switched to a March Brown. Then a Coachman. Nellie, beside me, began to get impatient. She went off downstream and began pulling at a stick. She ground it up and stripped it of bark. I told her I would be with her as soon as I had landed the fish.

The fish, if it existed, never bit. But time passed and when I looked up it was afternoon. That single hole, a gap in the rocks no wider than a welcome mat, had occupied me for a full hour. I found the entire episode puzzling, because every instinct told me a fish should have lived in the pool. At least one. But nothing did.

Finally I asked Nellie if she was ready to go. She looked at me expectantly, half-cocked to go in any direction I liked. "Ready," I asked her. "You ready?" Her eyes lifted and filled with attention. I teased her, asking which way she wanted to go. She grabbed the stick at her feet again and began to mangle it. When I finally pointed in the direction we had to go, she sprang out of the stream and headed downhill. I followed her. Long ago I had measured her against the breed characteristics promoted by the American Kennel Club. She was a handsome bitch, I knew, precisely the preferred height, twenty-one-and-a-half inches at the withers, and the proper color: lustrous white gold. Her forequarters were muscular and well coordinated, as the breed requirements stipulated, and her gait, as she trotted across the mountain vale, was well coordinated and powerful. Taken as a whole, she was a beautiful animal. I watched her with pleasure as she led me down the mountain.

Back at the truck, the packs smelled of fresh air and grass when I loaded them inside. I made Nellie stand on the tailgate while I brushed her. She let me do it for a long time, her grunts of satisfaction hearty and regular. As I finished, a family in a van pulled into the gravel slot beside the truck. Two children sat in the back, their heads barely visible above the door panels. The mom, a young, dark-haired woman, stared straight ahead. From the other side, a man stepped out from behind the wheel and took a picture of the mountains. When he finished, he asked about fishing, if I had had good luck, did I just arrive or was I done for the day. I told him I had slept out upstream the night before and he relayed the information to his children. They looked at me, one raising a hand to point to Nellie.

A second later, a large Chesapeake Retriever popped out of the van's side door. I hadn't seen it before. It was a huge animal, somewhat overfed, with a thick chest and an extremely abrupt stop where the snout built to the skull. It was also male as it made clear by circling around the lot and lifting its leg. The man who had taken the picture called it Chunky. Chunky the Chessie. The dog's collar clanked, as if its tags were made from tin license plates.

Nellie is not always friendly toward other dogs for reasons that are not clear to me. She doesn't attack, but she doesn't particularly overwhelm them with effusiveness. She growled as soon as she spotted Chunky. Chunky appeared oblivious, circling merrily and marking his turf. I called over to ask if Chunky was a friendly dog, and the owner replied that he was, too much so, and that Chunky had never fought with another dog. Nellie didn't agree. She growled steadily under my hand until I told her to quit it. Then Chunky resolved matters by coming to my truck and putting his flappy front paws on the tailgate. Nellie growled once, then shot out from under my hand. I held my breath, figuring I would have to separate them, but they had communicated something quicker than we could have guessed. Immediately they headed uphill, running shoulder to shoulder, their courtship apparently well advanced. The woman stepped out of the van and a second later the two kids, fraternal twins about seven years old, stepped out too. For a while we watched them run without saying anything.

Then the mom said that Chunky had a friend and it was difficult to deny that the two dogs had hit it off. They ran for the holy hell of it up and down the mountain, wrestling a little, but mostly running in a two-dog pack at top speed. Chunky was faster and larger; Nellie seemed to lead or at least establish direction. They only parted when they came to a bush or a tree, and then came back together as soon as they had passed that obstacle. I had never seen Nellie fall so hard for another dog. She had not run quite so freely, or so joyfully, since her puppy romps with Gusty.

We let them go. The mom, who introduced herself as Marion, offered me a brownie from a cake tin. They had just come from a visit with her sister in Cody. Now they were heading east. The kids, seeing the brownies, politely waited until she offered them one. They were great brownies. Jeff, the father, came around the van and looked at my truck. He said he had been to New Hampshire years ago, but hadn't been east of the Mississippi in at least a decade. He asked about the fishing. I told him where I had been, what I had been doing. Marion gave me another brownie and the kids split one. Unusual for Nellie, she did not keep an eye out for a potential treat. She ran a little more with Chunky, then waded in the water beside him, seemingly lovestruck.

Chunky, it turned out, was a working dog. The family ran a horse farm, a dude ranch, but Chunky was a gun dog who sometimes accompanied clientele on weekends. The farm had plenty of grouse and Chunky, despite appearances, was an excellent upland dog. He was also a good pet, Jeff told me, and Marion concurred. Chunky had gotten a little soft, they said, traveling the last few weeks. But he would get back into shape when they returned to their farm. Chunky had a busy life in Nebraska.

Finally the dogs came back and snaked around us, both of them wagging heavy tails. I was amazed at Nellie's flirtations. She didn't bother about the brownies or the chocolate gunk on the kids' hands, but continued circling, happy to be next to Chunky. I had never seen her behave in such a manner. For his part, Chunky seemed content to have her with him. He was a big dog, his back as wide as a bath towel. Nellie fit beside him nicely.

We stayed a little longer. Nellie didn't resist when I called her and told her to get in the truck. She hopped in, assuming the position she had taken for the last several weeks. We waved as we left. Chunky, by this time, had already climbed back in the van. I didn't see his head as we pulled out.

THE NORTH PLATTE

10:

IT'S STRANGE HOW OFTEN we can see something without taking it inside us. One Christmas morning my father sent me downstairs with wrapping paper and empty boxes three times before I noticed the new bicycle parked next to the garbage bin. He had parked it there the night before, but I had been so intent on getting rid of the wrapping paper—and getting back upstairs to play with my new toys—that I had passed over the bike twice before finally spotting it.

In much the same way, I discovered that Nellie's vision was failing. It became apparent to me as we stood on the banks of the North Platte deep in the Medicine Bow range, and once I knew, I realized I'd had telltale indications a hundred times before yet failed to note them. Now, standing downstream from me, she turned to look and her head stopped one, maybe two compass points from my exact location. Her tail wagged and her attention focused, but she did not see me. For an instant I waited, expecting her eyes to track in their swivel toward me, her head to turn more fully. Instead she seemed intent on the trees around me, as if she could not truly distinguish me. She recognized my voice, of course, and that brought her closer, but it was not until she approached me that finally she made me out. Then she ran forward, happy and less perplexed now that I was squarely in her vision, her tail waving above the river grass.

I propped my fly rod against a pine tree, then pulled her over and made her sit next to me. I kept my voice calm. From long association, I knew it was best to start any examination of her by petting. I gave her legs a rub, then worked my fingers into her chest hair. She grunted in satisfaction. It was a bright, sunny day and we sat for a while watching the water of the North Platte tumble over its rocky bed. I continued petting her until I was able to maneuver her face so that it pointed into the sunlight. Looking directly at her soft eyes, I saw nothing unusual, but when I turned her head to profile, two cataracts covered her corneas like pale blue moons.

Examining the size and dimension of the cataracts, I concluded that she had been losing her sight for some time. It had to be so. The cataracts did not look newly formed, whatever that meant exactly, and I did not think such things could come on suddenly like a rash or a swollen limb. The cataracts appeared firm and well established, clouds that had come for the serious business of blinding her. I studied them for awhile, nudging her chin this way and that. It was impossible to determine how much they affected her. She followed bird song and the few sounds squirrels made in the pines around us. Perhaps, though, she reconnoitered with her ears and relied on her nose, drawing on long habits of investigation. I thought of days when we had played Frisbee or ball for thirty minutes at a time, and surely she had seen those objects. She could still leap to catch a Frisbee or snatch a biscuit in the air if I lobbed it toward her.

Still, her vision had to be impaired. I wondered how long she had been following me by sound and smell and maybe by heart. She had hiked with me eleven miles into the Wind River Range, trusting me enough to follow blindly the cadence of my walking, the sound of my voice, trusting, as always, that her place was beside me.

I kept petting her and put my lips on her sunny head. It was a good day and her fur had taken on heat. I tried to recall what little I knew about cataracts, wondering at the same time if cataracts on dogs progressed the same way as cataracts on humans. My dad had cataracts, but I couldn't quite say how they settled on his eyes or what impact they had made in his life. He had died before they became an issue, although I was fairly certain he had consulted a surgeon about having them removed. In the back of my head I seemed to recall people saying that cataracts could be easily excised, but, like most medical procedures, such recipes mean little until you need one. I also remembered a childhood friend, Timmy Brown, whose dog spent his last years on a leash in the back yard, dozing in the sun. We had been warned repeatedly not to approach the dog—Chief, or Cricket was its name, I don't remember—because the dog had cataracts and might snap out of nervousness. The dog became a backyard dragon, a creature that haunted my nightmares. The sound of his chain evoked dragon scales, his bondage, to my over-stimulated imagination, the mythical restraint of a dark creature.

I petted Nellie for a while longer, then told her we had fish to catch. I told her she was a great dog, and I told her we had to live our fates no matter what. She waded into the water and splashed around, yanking at sticks as she likes to do. I figured that was as good an answer as she could make. I threw a stick downstream and let her splash up a storm retrieving it. She carried the stick to the bank and tore it up for the holy hell of it.

I had been casting on the North Platte most of the morning with no result, so I doubted her galloping through a few spots would make a difference. I didn't much care in any case. The North Platte was a surpassingly beautiful location, perhaps the best camping spot of any place I had visited. I had followed a long, winding dirt road through the Sheep Mountain Game Reserve, then ducked down, combing switchbacks against the side of a mountain, arriving finally on the banks of the North Platte. I carefully monitored weather reports throughout the trip, because I doubted I could make it out if a stiff snow fell. The Dakota only had rear-wheel drive, a stupid nod to economy I had regretted as soon as I purchased the truck. But I had arrived without incident and had set up an excellent camp twenty feet from the water so that I could have the sound of the river throughout the night. I had already gathered wood and set it beside the fire ring.

A clerk at a fly shop in Laramie had told me to fish upstream from the campground and I had followed his advice, though I suspected I hadn't walked far enough. I cast most of the morning with a bead-headed nymph to promising pockets, but no luck. Now, after lunch, I decided to fish one last afternoon, then call it a season.

Nellie led me upstream. She liked this place, I could tell. The air was crisp and small panes of ice had formed between the rocks along the shoreline. Now and then her paws shattered the ice and the noise carried out onto the river, then disappeared. We walked a few miles upstream, following game paths and the trails made by other anglers. When we came to an open meadow that roughly corresponded to the tip given me by the clerk in the fly shop, I began to fish. I decided to fish as carefully as I could, figuring that I would carry the memory of this day, for better or worse, through the long winter ahead.

The trick was to understand the water, I decided. Depth is signified by color in a river so I fished to black spots, the deeper places where trout should live. I used the sinking nymph and let it bump along the bottom. It was not particularly satisfying fishing, but after about twenty minutes a six-inch cutthroat hooked itself and jumped twice before I realized I had connected with it. Flecks of water splashed free from its body. I felt the fish in my wrists. Nellie nosed it when I landed it.

I thought about stopping on a good note. I considered returning to camp, pulling a beer out of the icy water where I had wedged it in the rocks beside the fire ring, but it was too early. Where one fish lives, many fish, any fish live, I recited. It was an old chant taught to me by an ancient man who used to fish the Wood River in Rhode Island. Before I caught a second fish, though, the sun tucked behind the mountains. When I looked up, I realized the river licked through the valley, a white gliding edge; for a moment I imagined the water not descending, but climbing instead, returning to the snow-topped peaks. I pictured the trout rising with the water, arching through pine and granite, gliding for a change instead of resisting. Maybe the trout buried themselves deep in the highest snow, their blood slowing until spring. Turtles, I knew, lived at the bottom of lakes, enzymes keeping their bodies from becoming ice. I liked thinking of the trout living a turtle's life, still, quiet, their gills stopped in mid-breath, their chins resting on the earth, waiting for April. I imagined them tumbling into the water in spring, the thaw a surprise, their bodies joyous as they rode the runoff back to their home waters.

No great moment marked the end of the season. I fished for a while longer and caught nothing. The six-inch cutthroat, it turned out, was my last trout. Winter, finally, had arrived. It came down the sides of the mountains and covered the river. Fog lifted off the stream. The fog hid Nellie as she walked me back to camp, then it took away the river and then the mountaintops.

I built a large fire. I am a fairly conscientious camper and don't often allow myself to indulge in large fires, but I had decided I was finished. I wanted a big fire with yellow flames. I grabbed a beer from the river and sat on the ground, my back propped against the float tube. The fire built slowly, then it took to the pine logs and climbed into the cool air. Nellie came to sit beside me. I tried to see her cataracts, the blue moons, but instead I received the wolf glow back—*tapetum lucidum*. I knew that dogs, like many animals, had a reflecting layer worked into their eyes that increased the acuity of vision during their optimum hunting hours at dawn and dusk. Such behavior, known as crepuscular activity as opposed to diurnal or nocturnal, was the boreal signature of wolves. I liked Nellie's wolf eyes. I told her so.

After a time and a few beers, I thought that I should do something to celebrate the end of the trip. I considered dancing around the fire or maybe dunking into one of the river's pools, or maybe stripping naked and running up a hillside, but I have never been one for theatrics. I piled more wood on the fire and watched the sparks go off into the night. I kept Nellie next to me. I thought of Wendy, the woman in my life, and her son, Pie. Wendy and I had begun to talk about throwing our hats in together, buying a house and getting on with things. It had been years since I had even considered living with a woman.

Around eight I stopped feeding the fire and started carrying coffeepotfuls of water to douse the ashes. As soon as the fire quit, I began to shiver. We climbed into the truck and performed what was by then an old routine. This time, though, I left the tailgate down and I pulled the sleeping mat out so that I had an unobstructed view of the stars. I read Dylan Thomas's lines from *A Winter's Tale:*

> And the stars falling cold,
> And the smell of hay in the snow, and the far owl
> Warning among the folds, and the frozen hold
> Flocked with the sheep white smoke of the farm house cowl
> In the river wended vales where the tale was told.

I extinguished the flashlight and let my eyes adjust to the darkness. I pulled Nellie closer, up under the sleeping bag, and I pet her slowly. The river pressed close to the bank and I listened for owls but didn't hear one.

I packed in first light while Nellie ate and took care of her morning chores. I had traveled enough through the years to know that once you turn for home every delay becomes unbearable. The scenery that had seemed novel and interesting a month or two before suddenly turns dull and lifeless, becomes an obstacle keeping you from where you want to be. As I loaded the truck, my mind had already gone to details about stacking wood and getting the snow blower primed. I calculated five hundred miles a day, then divided it into the miles between me and home. Three days, I figured, if my luck held. Four on the outside.

Before we finished packing, a cowboy appeared. He came out of the woods on a tall horse, ten or twenty head of cattle scattered before him. I put Nellie in a down-stay and told her to hold steady. The cowboy raised his hand and guided his horse toward me. The cattle moved slowly, stopping frequently to graze. Nellie watched, her attention fixed on them. They appeared thinner than the eastern cattle I was accustomed to seeing. They made a lot of noise and smelled like hay.

The cowboy introduced himself as Jim. He had spent the last two days picking up strays, he told me, driving them slowly toward the trailhead up the road. The cattle grazed on public lands, he said, but ran in front of the snow once it started to settle on the high country. He was to be met by livestock trucks later in the day, then a day off, then more riding.

"You from around here?" I asked.

"Ohio," he said and laughed.

His uncle knew the cattle rancher and had arranged a job for him, Jim, as something of a life experience. Jim had always wanted to try the cowboy life. As confidently as he moved on the horse, it surprised me when he said he had only ridden a few times previously. The rancher had thrown him on a horse, given him a bedroll, and told him to go find strays. It had been one of the best experiences in his life, he said. He wouldn't trade it for anything, though he was cured of wanting a cowboy's existence.

"It's the cold, mostly," he said. "That's what gets you. The rest of it is okay but it's so damned cold."

"You sleep out?" I asked.

He nodded, said, "It's okay because I have a good sleeping bag, but you wonder what it would have been like before they invented down bags."

He asked if I was elk hunting or fishing and nodded again when I told him. When I said I was heading off east, he said that he had been out my way once, years ago, to look at the fall foliage. His mom had taken him. He remembered it as staying a long time in a car and looking out the window. He wasn't certain he had visited New Hampshire, though he thought he had. He said up around Lake Erie they had fall foliage a lot like New England.

I told him he should try a lobster boat for his next job and he laughed. After saying good-bye he turned his horse's head and wandered back to the cattle, his return enough to get them moving again. I kept Nellie in a down-stay until they disappeared down the road. Then it was time to go.

When we started up the switchbacks, I glanced at Nellie. As usual she sat with her nose an inch from the windshield, dotting her nostril print on the glass whenever we stopped or started. I wondered, as I studied her, if she knew we had started for home. *Heading home,* I whispered to her but she didn't react. I wondered if she knew where we had been, why we had gone, what any of it meant. For the heck of it, I made her give me her paw in return for a biscuit. I wanted to see if she was listening so I said, "dog," which got her looking left and right, trying to see a potential adversary. Then I had to devote my attention to driving the switchbacks and I let her be. She watched out the window. We drove on the dirt road until we reached a paved road, then drove the paved road until we reached a bigger road. By afternoon we saw the Rockies shrink in the rearview mirror, and I realized, things go as they might, that Nellie would never see them again.

HAMPSHIRE 11:
NEW

I SCHEDULED AN APPOINTMENT for Nellie the week I returned. The receptionist asked after the reason for the appointment, and I told her that Nellie had undergone surgery in the spring, and added that her eyes, from what I could tell, had grown cataracts. The receptionist noted the information and confirmed the time. She also checked Nellie's record and said she could receive a global booster shot and give a blood sample for heartworm. The appointment would be in three days. We spent the interval moving back into the house, setting up things for winter. I took the snowblower to the local hardware store to have it serviced. I bought pumpkins and squash and ordered holiday pies. Nellie accompanied me on my rounds, her position in the truck as steady as it had been out West. The best foliage was already spent.

The night before the appointment we made a fire and sat beside it for most of the evening. I went through mail and burned off envelopes and junk. Nellie stretched out on a braided rug near the hearth and moved only to get the heat from a new direction. When I bent over to pet her, as I did occasionally, her fur felt warm and soft. Each time I stepped over to add a log to the fire, I rubbed her with my socked foot on the return.

She stayed by the fire until long after I had gone to bed, but I heard her creep onto the mattress in the darkness. I reached down to pet her and her tail thumped a few times on the comforter. The wind coming under the sash did not feel or taste the same as the breezes had in April. I told Nellie winter was coming. I told her we could have snow any day. I tickled her behind the ear, then fell asleep to a late storm pattering on the roof.

The next day, I spent the earliest part of the morning cleaning my office at school. It was choked with papers and student essays. I kept Nellie on an L.L Bean bed next to my desk. She likes coming to my office because it gives her a chance to be social, and students, I find, appreciate the companionship of a dog. She watched as I carted out boxes of papers and memos to the dumpster behind the dorms. It was a dark day and we worked with the lights on even at nine in the morning. I spent an hour answering phone messages and writing a long, difficult student recommendation. Near ten a student came in with a convoluted excuse of why he hadn't registered for a course in the spring, and why it was necessary that he get in. As he told me his story Nellie kept her chin on his knee.

We made it to Dr. Sweet's office at noon. The office smelled of chicken soup. We read copies of *Dog Fancier* and *Field and Stream* until Dr. Sweet's assistant called us to the examination room. Nellie made one yank for the door, determined that she wasn't going to escape, then calmly followed. Dr. Sweet entered a moment later, his standard blue smock clean and bright. Together we hoisted Nellie onto the examination table, a steel shelf protruding from the wall. It's a measure of her patience and trust that she didn't protest.

Dr. Sweet asked how she was doing. I said okay. I said I thought I'd found lumps once more, but they didn't feel substantial and seemed to have gone away. He said I should remain vigilant. He took an otoscope and shined it beneath her floppy ears, then checked her gums. He felt around her legs and in her gut for lumps. He listened to her heart, took her temperature, then patted her rump. Finally he inspected her eyes.

I had learned more about cataracts since returning from our trip. Clouding, or keratitis, is a fairly common occurrence in dogs over ten years old, I had read. Aging produces a gradual clouding of the lens (sclerosis). Cataracts and luxated lenses are only surgically removed when the surgery will result in substantially improved vision. Old dogs get along surprisingly well with reduced eyesight. They rely on other senses and adapt, as we all must, to the limitations of age. Nellie, to be sure, had not slowed substantially. Except for an occasional lapse in her perceptions, she seemed as solid as ever.

"Looks good all around," Dr. Sweet said when he finished with her eyes. "Is she having any problem seeing?"

"Not that I can tell. Nothing very dramatic."

"I guess we'll let well enough alone, then," he said. "There's not much to be done about it."

He asked about her appetite, about her exercise, then grabbed a syringe and gave her a shot. He took a blood sample for spring heartworm. That was it. She was certified healthy for another six months. We paid on the way out. Nellie was halfway through her twelfth year.

Outside in the truck, I pulled Nellie onto my lap. I held her against my chest and put my lips against her fur. She smelled like pine and faintly, very faintly, of the puppy she had been. Lake swimmer, I whispered to her. Frisbee catcher. I put my eyes against her fur and felt such tenderness toward her that I was afraid to lift my face from her shoulder. I pictured her running across the mountainside near the Tongue River, her fur shining, her gait impeccable, and I squeezed her harder. I felt the deep, convulsive grind toward a sob, but then I pushed it away. She was all right. She would be all right for a while longer.

At home we took a walk in the woods. Our routine is to enter the forest directly behind my house. Nellie knows the path and sprints ahead. She is always glad to be out for a walk and she usually runs the beginning portion of the trail with her nose to the ground, her back legs catapulting her forward. A half mile along the path we struck Clay Brook where Nellie loves to lap up the icy water. This day the trees and wind made little noise. I don't think Nellie noticed. She had curled into the boggy area to the south, though she was still within sight. I stood next to the stream and watched her run through the dark afternoon. She seemed unconscious of me. She ran on a game trail, a place where we sometimes found deer rubbings and bear scat, her impatient body occasionally striking the staghorn sumac and making their red heads wag in the quiet.

In February Wendy and I and her eight-year-old son, Pie, put a down payment on a converted barn in northern New Hampshire with a view overlooking Mt. Moosilauke. It is a wonderful structure, a post-and-beam barn built around 1840. The roof rises four stories tall and contains a nine-foot-wide chimney made of gray quarry stone. On the Fourth of July the town fire department shoots off fireworks that land on the open meadow rolling out from a wide farmer's porch on the east end of the building. We have already planned a party for the Fourth of July and invited chili recipes. We have spent days going to auctions and flea markets, searching for furniture and interesting pieces to use in decorating. Both Wendy and I have been accustomed to small homes and apartments, and now, suddenly, we have more space than we know what to do with. Pie talks about hooking a rope up to the top beam of the barn and swinging like Tarzan down to breakfast.

The barn land connects to an ancient Baltimore & Ohio rail bed, which connects, in turn, to the Appalachian Trail. Since we returned, Nellie and I now walk with a second dog, Devil Dog, the small black Lab who belongs to Pie. Devil Dog is five and has the springy, short body of a well-proportioned Lab. She weighs fifty pounds to Nellie's seventy, but she is muscular, with a broad chest and well-defined legs. She is a nearly perfect pet, with a shy, affable way, and a goofy love of water.

I was curious to see how Nellie would accept another dog's presence and was not surprised when she remained aloof at first. For a month or more she pretended Devil Dog did not exist. But Devil Dog, or D Dog as we call her, is a determined clown and I think she spotted at once that Nellie takes herself very seriously. D Dog is the annoying, yet necessary, little sister, the type who refuses to let Nellie hog the toys and the attention. She also seeks Nellie out at night and curls next to her, forcing Nellie to share her dog bed. I suspect it will keep Nellie lively to have a younger dog in the house. On our walks, Nellie is still dominant, still the adventurer, while D Dog remains close underfoot, manic only when Nellie returns.

My life has changed. On my walks now I return to a lighted house and a wood stove heating a keeping room. Better still, I now have human company on my walks. On Sundays we schedule hikes and take off to new destinations. We have discovered a waterfall we believe no one knows exists except us, a rock formation we have dubbed Elephant Rock, and a swimming hole that is so cold Pie believes the water comes to us from the time of the cavemen, which is the highest praise he can give to anything. We have set up a specimen shelf and bring back fossils, birds' nests, and pale blue mermaid tears. Pie carries the things to second grade Show & Tell where he delivers wonderfully garbled accounts of the origins of such things, mixing fact and fancy as it strikes him.

Our biggest find to date has been a moose leg. Nellie found it. I was on a walk alone with her when she appeared in the path ahead of me, a moose hock in her mouth. The shin still wore the skin of a moose and the massive hoof, curved like the horned calipers of a gigantic beetle, dangled with an articulated wobble next to Nellie's chest. The sight of Nellie with such a large object stopped me. It was shocking, but also decidedly fascinating. I fought the impulse to junk it and carried it, by a handhold of leaves, back for Pie to inspect. He put it in his tree fort to decompose, following a stern recommendation from his mom. Like a ghoulish imp he checks on it regularly and loves to haul it down to show visitors. When anyone from out of state mentions the difficulty of seeing a moose, Pie and I wink and he clambers off like a young Quasimodo to fetch his moose leg. We never fail to think it's funny.

On the fourth Saturday of April, opening day for trout waters, it's my habit to strap a float tube to my back and hike into one particular pond I know. I did it this past spring. The night before, I set out my equipment, much of it still musty from the fall. I have made it a tradition to start the new season with the last fly of the old season, and I found the bead-headed nymph I had last used on the North Platte. It appeared in pretty good shape. I dabbed oil on my reel sprockets, checked my leaders, threw out a few old flies, went through the pockets of my fly jacket, checked the retractable thingy on my jacket chest pocket to make sure I still had clippers and forceps, stuck a new can of Deep Woods Off in the back game pouch, and then packed it all in my pickup.

I woke at four the next morning and slipped out of the house with Nellie beside me. We drove to the trailhead and arrived as the sun cleared the White Mountains. It was cold, only forty-some degrees, but I knew the hike would warm me. We started up Guinea Pond Trail at 5:30. Nellie took the lead. The float tube bobbed against my back and made it hard, because of its width, to pass between trees. Before I had hiked fifteen minutes my body had heated. I kept my pace steady, glad to be outside.

It was a five-mile hike to Black Mountain Pond. Nellie flushed a grouse on the way. I heard the first wood thrush of the season. Its call sounded like water seeping through glass. I love the sound and wait for it each year. When we arrived at the pond, I drank some coffee and ate a sandwich I had packed. I gave Nellie a biscuit and told her to stand guard on the bank. She looked dubious, but contented herself with sniffing around old fire rings and inspecting the spring skunk cabbage.

The trout in Black Mountain Pond are small—five to six inch brookies, known locally as square tails. The pond itself rests at about two thousand feet in a bowl of piney hills. The

mountains sometimes reflect in the water and the clouds, passing above, glide from peak to peak.

After breakfast I climbed into my gear and backed into the
water. Nellie found a rock in the early sun and rested. I clicked
out my line and began to cast near a row of lily pads. The bead-
headed nymph made a satisfying kerplunk when it hit the
water. After about fifteen or twenty casts, a brookie took. It
surged for a moment downward, heading to the center of the
earth, but the line danced him up and to the surface and eventually he burbled in the glassy reflection of the pond. I lifted my
rod tip and brought him close. The red dots along his side held
the color of sugar maples turning at first frost.

But it was spring and the fish began to rise in the fresh lily
pads, one after another. I squinted to see what they might be
feeding on, but it was hard to tell. I thought maybe a March
Brown. I thought it could be a small dun. Either way, I doubted
the trout would be especially choosy. I cast the nymph to the
edge of the lily pads and caught another. The fish ran straight at
me and passed close to my legs. I pivoted in the water and let
the trout head to the center of the pond, then let it turn back to
me when it felt the leader.

Nellie came out before I caught a third fish. I didn't see her
leave the shore, but she paddled out to the float tube, her head
a wedge above the water. She came close and I stuck out a foot
to fend her off, because I knew she would want to climb up with
me. No, I said, grinning. She circled me for ten minutes, which
of course interfered with my fishing. It did no good to tell her to
wait on shore. After a while I waited until she was on the side
away from the lily pads, then I cast quickly. I caught two fish
that way with Nellie banking around me, a satellite, a comet.
She seemed happy.

It was only ten in the morning when I climbed out and made a fire. I was cold, bone cold, and my fingers trembled when I held the match to the cotton ball swabbed in petroleum jelly I use to start fires in the woods. Because I was one of the first visitors to the pond that season, I had no difficulty finding dead wood. I snapped off small twigs and built the fire with dry, splintered pine. It crackled happily. I held out my hands and tried to get feeling back in my toes. Nellie sat beside me, her fur icy at its tips.

I fished from the shore in the afternoon, but didn't have much luck. I caught one nice trout on a Muddler Minnow. I had seen a few black grasshoppers working the early grasses at the side of the pond, and on a hunch I had tied on a black Muddler and cast it to imitate the real thing. A large trout took almost immediately. The fish pulled heavily and nearly wrapped itself around a partially submerged log. The trout shook free when it was inches from me, gone back to the water before I understood exactly what had occurred.

It was a fish to end on. I reeled in and packed up my rod, the float tube, my fly jacket. I gave Nellie a few biscuits and told her to get ready. When I had hoisted everything onto my back, we started down the mountain. As always, Nellie led me. Her tail wagged above her back and her gait, swift and clean, looked as strong as it ever had. I thought of a day when she would not be ahead of me on the trail, but that was a gloomy thought, not one for today. She had several more seasons in her. The trees misted green buds from their limbs and water ran happily through the forest. It was spring, and trout had returned, as they promised to every fall, and I had met them again. The summer was ahead, then autumn, and in each season the water waited. That was what counted. In the late afternoon I knew Wendy

189

and I would split wood, and Pie would play with the dogs, and we would sleep with the windows open to catch the wind from the mountains. Nellie would sleep still curled at the foot of the bed, able to rest after so many days afield because she had retrieved me, brought me home at last.

ACKNOWLEDGMENTS

I AM GRATEFUL TO ALL THOSE WHO READ THE MANUSCRIPT of this particular work and generously gave their time and insight. I am particularly indebted to Tim Weed and Wendy Hast for their commentary and encouragement. Thanks to Jay Schaefer, senior editor, and the wonderful staff at Chronicle Books for producing this book. I am enormously grateful to Jennifer Hengen, my agent at Sterling-Lord Literistic, for her many kindnesses to me. Thanks, too, to Dr. Dennis Sweet for his care of Nellie; and to Kelly Bryer, who has groomed Nellie for ten years. And finally, my thanks to Nellie herself, a good companion and a good dog all these years. I hope that I have been the friend to her that she has been to me.

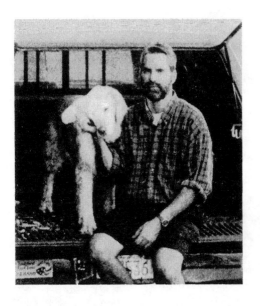

Joseph Monninger is the author of eight novels, as well as numerous stories and articles. He lives and teaches in New Hampshire.

Printed in the United States
by Baker & Taylor Publisher Services